THE SORROW

THE SORROWFUL WAY

The Mind of Christ,
the Path of Discipleship
and the Christian Year

—

MICHAEL PERHAM

First published in Great Britain in 1998 by
SPCK, Marylebone Road, London NW1 4DU

ACKNOWLEDGEMENTS

The publisher acknowledges with thanks permission to reproduce extracts
from the following publications:

Extracts from *The Alternative Service Book 1980, Lent, Holy Week,
Easter* (1984, 1986) and *The Promise of His Glory* (1990, 1991) are
copyright © The Central Board of Finance of the Church of England
and are reproduced by permission.
James Quinn, 'God is love', © Geoffrey Chapman, an imprint of Cassell plc.
Bill Vanstone, 'Love's Endeavour, Love's Expense'. Reproduced by
permission of J. W. Shore.
Edwin le Grice, 'Image of the Eternal Father'. Copyright by
Kevin Mayhew Ltd. Used by permission Licence No. 798002.
Elizabeth Jennings, 'Bread', *In the Meantime*, © Carcanet Press, 1996.
Elizabeth Jennings, 'Christ's Agony in the Garden', *Consequently I Rejoice*,
© Carcanet Press, 1977.
Dorothy L. Sayers, *The Just Vengeance*, © Gollancz, 1946.
R. S. Thomas, 'Kneeling', *Selected Poems 1946–1968*,
© Bloodaxe Books Ltd, 1986.
W. H. Auden, 'At the Manger Mary sings', *Collected Longer Poems*,
© Faber & Faber, 1968.
T. S. Eliot, 'The Journey of the Magi', *Collected Poems 1909–1962*,
© Faber and Faber, 1963.
T. S. Eliot, *Murder in the Cathedral*, © Faber and Faber, 1935.

Bible quotations are from the New Revised Standard Version
of the Bible © 1989.

The verses on pages 25, 69, 88, 94 and 96 are written by the author.

British Library Cataloguing-in-Publication Data
A catalogue record for this book is available from the British Library

ISBN 0-281-05131-3

Photoset by David Gregson Associates, Beccles, Suffolk
Printed in Great Britain by The Cromwell Press, Trowbridge, Wiltshire

For Alison
with love and gratitude

CONTENTS

PREFACE

The Sorrowful Way is about Christian discipleship and about the mystery of being 'conformed to the image of Christ'. It does this in relation to the feasts and seasons of the Christian year from Christmas to Easter. So there is a liturgical dimension to the book. But it is not a liturgical handbook. It is the attempt of one priest to make sense of a central theme of the Christian faith through a series of reflections that turned into sermons and then into the written word. Because I am a liturgist, the way in is often through the liturgy, and indeed part of what I have wanted to do is to show how, for me at least, the liturgy often is the way into the heart of Christian truth and experience. Yet, in the end, it is belief and discipleship, not liturgy, that is my concern in this book.

Most of its chapters received their first public hearing as independent sermons and addresses. But none of them appears in its original form, and some have been considerably reworked. Yet each one can still stand on its own, despite the common theme that runs through the whole book. Although it is often thought to be a compliment to a book when the reviewer or the reader cannot put it down, I believe this book would best be read with a certain amount of putting down between chapters. It could be read as a continuous whole and there is intended to be a progression through its pages. But it is not a book for a single sitting. There is something to be said for reading it over the weeks and months of the Christian year that it covers from Christmas to Easter.

Some chapters began life as a series of Good Friday addresses for St Paul's Church Weeke in Winchester. The majority were written as sermons for St George's Oakdale, where I was team rector from 1984 to 1992, or for Norwich Cathedral, where I have served since 1992. Individual chapters had their origins in sermons at St Mary's Addington, St John's Winchester and St George's Cathedral Perth. Chapter 1 is newly written.

Whenever a preacher writes a sermon, there is much indebtedness to other writers and other preachers, as well as to the community whose particular concerns or needs have led to the sermon. I readily acknowledge all these debts. I am particularly conscious that Chapter 3, 'How Long they had Waited', was written and preached only a few days after hearing a sermon in Salisbury Cathedral by Dean Hugh Dickinson. Although, in the end, my own sermon developed in a different direction and moved towards a different point, I remember that his sermon was directly the inspiration for my own and used some of his imagery. I am grateful for that inspiration, as for many others who have been the means by which new thoughts have come into my mind.

Half way through the book comes a chapter, 'Finding the True Cross', rather different in style from the others. In the other chapters I have tried to remove the reliance of the sermon on the particular church community and building in which it was preached. But Chapter 7 makes sense only by reference to the art and architecture of Norwich Cathedral and to my own relationship to it. I have left it in that more personal contextualized form. I have also left it with its description of chapels and their paintings as they were when the sermon was preached in 1994, and not as some of them are today.

I record my thanks to those kind people who encouraged me to turn sermons and addresses into a book, to my colleagues in the Dean and Chapter of Norwich who, by granting me sabbatical leave for eight weeks, created the space in which that process could happen, to Rachel Boulding, then at SPCK, for her enthusiasm for the project, and to my wife, Alison, to whom the book is dedicated, and whose influence for good on what I preach and write is, I suspect, greater than either of us usually acknowledges.

Michael Perham

Norwich
1997

Dream. In human dreams earth ascends to Heaven
Where no one need pray nor ever feel alone.
In your first few hours of life here, O have you
Chosen already what death must be your own?
How soon will you start on the Sorrowful Way?
Dream while you may.

W. H. Auden

1

CONFORMED TO THE IMAGE
OF HIS SON

To be a Christian is both the simplest thing in the world and also the work of a lifetime. For to be a Christian is to put one's trust in Jesus Christ as Saviour and Lord. Millions of Christians have put it as straightforwardly as that. And, at one level, that is all that needs to be said. Sometimes the putting of one's trust happens in a flash of recognition in a single moment. Sometimes it is an almost unconscious daily reaffirmation of a trusting that has always been there. In either case to recognize that Jesus holds the key to life and to death, to living and believing, to earth and heaven, is fundamental for the Christian. However little that sense of trust may be articulated, however uncertain and unformed the theology that lies behind it, to believe that about Jesus, to see in him both the clue to God and the path to God, is to be a Christian.

But it is also the work of a lifetime, because the first thing that Jesus says to any disciple – not just to a first-century fisherman mending his nets or a tax collector at his desk, but to any disciple in any age – is 'Follow me' (Mark 1.17). The Gospels record how, with a magnetism that still surprises, Jesus so challenged those first disciples that Andrew and Simon, James and John, and Matthew soon after, took him very literally, simply left what they were doing, and began to walk with him. But his 'Follow

1

me' was never, even for them, a once-for-all invitation. The following was not achieved, only begun, when they left their nets, their tax forms or their families. Again and again he had to keep saying it, this 'Follow me' that after a while acquired a sterner and less attractive tone, an invitation to 'take up your cross and follow me' (Mark 8.34).

What did it mean to follow Christ as they did? There are moments in the Gospels when it is as if the Lord strides ahead and the role of the disciples is quite literally to follow, to struggle to keep up. There can be a kind of blind loyalty that cannot begin to understand what the master is up to, or what is motivating him, but which trusts and follows. Or there can be the kind of trust that simply finds a warm security in placing one's steps in the master's footprints. But, if the relationship of the Christian to Jesus is one of disciple to teacher, a different kind of engagement is normally required. The disciple, the follower, needs to enter into the mind of the teacher, to begin at least to make sense of where he is leading and why. And so the picture the Gospels portray is more usually of Jesus and his disciples walking together, but also talking together. He wants them to understand, though the evangelists sometimes fear that they are destined not to do so.

'Teaching' is sometimes a rather strong word for what Jesus is doing. Certainly there are the set-piece teaching scenes for the great crowds. Yet more often there is the sense of the man who shares sufficient of himself, his hopes, his motivation, that some of it at least rubs off on those who have thrown in their lot with him. And there are moments when their understanding seems to leap forward. Or, at very least, there are moments when the walking stops, sometimes even the talking too, and something happens. Something happens which they may not understand, but they know it to be charged with significance, though the meaning will take its time to dawn upon them. They come to a mountain, for instance, and some of them go up with him, and there follows just such a moment, charged with significance, as a cloud descends, a voice speaks and glory is almost tangible. Peter is still reflecting on it, articulating the meaning, years on.

> For we did not follow cleverly devised myths, when we made known to you the power and coming of our Lord Jesus Christ, but we had been eye witnesses of his majesty. For he received honour and glory from God the Father, when that voice was conveyed to him by the Majestic Glory, saying, 'This is my Son, my Beloved, with whom I am well pleased.' We ourselves heard this voice come from the heaven, while we were with him on the holy mountain (2 Peter 1.16–18).

It is the same with the Holy Week walking. They enter the city amidst the palms and hosannas on Sunday and move in and out of it over the next few days until the journey brings them all on Thursday to a particular house, with an upper room. He takes bread and wine. There is a kind of hush, and the talking now is not conversation, but a revelatory word from the Lord that will enter deeply into the Christian memory: 'This is my body which is given for you. This is my blood which is shed for you.'[1] It is another of those moments charged with significance, another of those moments in which discipleship is formed.

There is another three evenings later, when the disciples, returning to Emmaus, engage in that familiar (yet on this occasion strangely different and for a while unfamiliar) walking and talking. Again it leads to a meal. Here we are not told what words were spoken, but it is another moment charged with significance, and this time the meaning does not take long to dawn.

Between those two experiences of disclosure, when those who had walked with Jesus stopped, listened, looked and found their experience of discipleship changed, stands the cross. The disciples had apparently heard more than once that this was where following him would lead. This, of course, was the moment charged with greatest significance, and here more than anywhere else it took time for the meaning to emerge. Indeed these disciples who had done their best to follow could have learned no instant lesson about its significance, for they had run away. Admittedly the knowledge that they ran away when faced with the cross was in itself, of course, part of the formation of their discipleship, but only later would greater truths emerge. Later they did indeed make sense of the cross. It was, as Paul helped them to see, the 'power of God and the wisdom of God' (1 Corinthians 1.24). Initially they could not see that. Even the evangelists were puzzled about the traditions of what Jesus had said as he hung there, where the walking had ended on the Hill of the Skull. For all that we try to make sense of the words they record him saying, we know that his silence speaks at that moment more tellingly than his words.

Christian discipleship through the centuries has not, like that of Andrew and Simon and James and Matthew, run away from the cross. It has stared at it and tried to make sense of it. It has puzzled over the meaning of 'taking up the cross and following' Christ. Sometimes it has simply been perplexed by it. Sometimes it has been content simply to gaze, adore, give thanks, trust unquestioningly. But, more often, Christian people, focusing on the man hanging there, have tried to understand. They have wanted to know what makes him tick. They have wanted to get inside his mind. More even than that (for the one who hangs there is flesh and blood) they have wanted to get inside his skin.

4

They have seen the need to do this because they have recognized that, when Christ is not the physical presence striding ahead or the companion engaging them in the conversation that he was for the first disciples, to follow him involves above all else a kind of identification with him. To follow, in Christian terms, is not to trail a little behind, but to walk precisely the same path, and to do it with the same conviction. For Christian formation is a process by which the Holy Spirit moulds us to Christ's shape, conforms us to his pattern. It is this that, for most of us, is the work of a lifetime. We are committed to it the moment we respond to the invitation to follow him. In baptism, with all its rich theology of living and dying with Christ, we accept that pattern, the life-style of Christ. But appropriating it, making it our own, is a more complex and lengthy business, and the Spirit's work of moulding us into the shape of Christ is hardly ever straightforward. 'Moulding' may seem too gentle a word for what sometimes needs to happen; 'knocking into shape' may be nearer the mark.

This pattern to which we are committed by our baptism is fundamental to Christian discipleship. Yet people often fail to see the point. It is for them as if trust and faith in Jesus, linked perhaps with an overwhelming gratitude to him, can insure against the challenges and trials of life. But in the end the vocation of the Christian is to go with the challenges and the trials, to see them through the eyes of Christ, to engage with them as he engaged; in other words, to be conformed to his pattern, his image. As Paul puts it in the Letter to the Romans:

> For those whom he foreknew he also predestined to be conformed to the image of his Son, in order that he might be the firstborn within a large family (8.29).

And in the Letter to the Philippians:

> I want to know Christ and the power of his resurrection, and the sharing of his sufferings by becoming like him in his death, if somehow I may attain the resurrection from the dead (3.10).

The Authorized Version of the Bible speaks here of 'being made conformable with his death', and that expresses more strongly this sense of identification that begins in baptism but is the work of a lifetime.

To follow in Christ's way and be conformed to his pattern is not simply a matter of imitating his death, though it is in his passion that our identification with him is at its most formative. We enter into his mind, as far as we are able, in order to follow him through all the emotions of human existence. We share his joy, his faith, his easy relationship with the Father, his touches of humour, his capacity for friendship, his riding high, just as much as we identify with his pain, his isolation, his doubt and, in the end, the fragility of his faith. The message of the Gospels is that the whole story from birth to death and on to resurrection is a complex interweaving of all these aspects of human life. The way of the cross and the way of life and peace turn out, not so much to run in parallel, but to be a single path. But to that we will return. Sufficient to say here that to follow Christ, to be conformed to his image, is to enter imaginatively into his mind and heart, and sometimes even into his body.

It is important to say 'enter imaginatively'. Biblical scholarship has warned us through this century against a foolish search for a kind of biographical picture of an historical Jesus of whom we can speak with confident detail. It is a legitimate approach to Scripture to use it imaginatively and creatively, to let its pictures interact with our experience and our own longings, but we need to be wary lest we think we shall ever quite fathom the mind of Jesus Christ. Yet the story we tell of him – the words the Scriptures attribute to him (even when they almost contradict each other, as the words from the cross in the different Gospels very nearly do) and the images the Church has developed of him – engages with our story, in such a way that our own humanity becomes the more intelligible to us. In that revelation about ourselves we may trust to know more of him and more also of his Father. Through the story told of him we learn more of our own story. Through our own story, told with integrity, we perceive some of the truth about him, and even catch a glimpse of the divine.

This has always been the Christian vocation. It is part of the timeless meaning of baptism. But there is a sense in which it may be more difficult in today's world for some people to make it their own. There has always been pain and suffering in the world and no one is quite exempt from it. In our own contemporary world there is as much suffering as ever, and the record of the twentieth century is one of evil, pain and suffering on a scale that has undermined faith both in God and in the human race. Yet, for all that, in our Western culture we are more able to protect ourselves from some aspects of suffering than any civilization before us. We can alleviate pain in a way that has seldom happened before. We have created escape routes from conditions of life that oppress and deaden and sadden, where in the past we would simply have endured. Fewer of us than in the past come face to face with death as part of normal existence; when we do come across it we are protected from some of its most shocking aspects. Even our religious beliefs are more comfortable and less distressing than those of our forebears.

Much of that is good, but it may not help us to be conformed to the pattern of Christ that turns out to be the path of salvation. Although there are some Christians in our Western society who know exactly what it means to suffer with Christ, and even to go under when the suffering is intolerable, there are many whom life has treated so gently and smoothly that, almost guiltily, they cannot claim to walk in the way of the cross with any real knowledge of its weight and its cost. How may they follow Christ with integrity and find themselves moulded into his shape?

I believe that one of the answers – and among many answers it is the one that I want to pursue in these pages – is that they may be formed in their Christian discipleship and moulded into his shape by the liturgy of the Church and in particular by the celebration of the Christian year. The celebration of the Christian year, in its succession of feasts and fasts and seasons, brings before us the story of Jesus. It places it within the context of worship in such a way that people may reflect and explore and, crucially, make connections between that story and their own, or between that story and the story of those who suffer today. Bit by bit, year by year, we are enabled in retelling the story, through the words and songs and symbols of its annual cycle, to go a little deeper, to enter more profoundly into the mind of Christ. Though our assimilation of it may sometimes leap forward in a great bound, more often it is a gradual and almost imperceptible process of growing into Christ.

Within that process someone who has been going through a great trauma (whether bereavement or loss of faith or mental illness or unrelenting physical pain) may be helped little by little to work it through, to discover a Christ-like way to respond to their trauma. Within that process somebody else who feels that their life is too easy and shallow may be given the insight, by entering into the experience of Christ, to enter also into the sufferings of those around them in a way they could not do before. Within that process another set of people may learn enough of the way of Christ such that when, one day in the future, they are faced with a crisis unlike anything they have known before, their response will be instinctively Christ-like.

This Christ-like way is not, of course, a resilient rising above every trauma and crisis. But nor is it a kind of fatalistic going under in the face of loss or pain or fear. The way of Christ goes with events, not exactly rising above them or being dragged down by them, but going on being open and alive through them, creative through them, integrity intact, even if faith sometimes fails. That is the pattern of Christ.

Here is work for a lifetime, and the liturgy plays its part in conforming us to the image of Christ. In the chapters that follow we look through the cycle of the Christian year at the story of Christ, from his birth at Bethlehem to the rebirth of the resurrection, and find it to be a sorrowful way, even from the beginning, but a story that spells salvation none the less.

2

LED ALL THAT WAY
FOR BIRTH OR DEATH?

Christmas and Epiphany

The liturgy of Christmas midnight takes the ministers first to the crib. Christmas Eve is always a busy day for clergy and lay people alike, rushing around in last minute preparations and, in cathedrals and churches themselves, much getting ready for the festival and several services to punctuate the day. And then, as midnight approaches, to enter the church, packed full of eager worshippers, and to make for the crib, is to be faced with the heart of the Christmas message. There may be the shepherds and those inevitable props of the Christmas scene – star and straw, ox and ass and lamb – and certainly there will be faithful Joseph with the mother and the new-born child. There are prayers to be said, everyone turned towards the crib. Only those very near can see, but all can visualize, for there is no more familiar scene in all the Christian story. For those who stand close to the crib there is the chance to gaze and to be humbled. But the prayers are soon over and *Gloria in excelsis Deo* rings out from the choir, *Gloria in excelsis Deo et in terra pax*, 'Glory to God in the highest and on earth peace'. The procession moves away from the crib as the song of the angels is sung, 'Glory to God in the highest'. Yes, it is to God's glory, God's alone, that the Christmas song is sung.

10

Consider for a moment the central figures in the drama of Christmas night. First there is Mary; Mary in the crib and Mary on a million Christmas cards. We need not be deceived by the calm, serene composure of the Virgin as we portray her in paint or wood or stone. For all her serenity, here is a woman of suffering. There has been the malicious gossip as she grows bigger in her pregnancy. There has been that long, long journey to Bethlehem where there was no room for them in the inn. There has been the pain of childbirth, in a stable, in sight of ox and ass and within earshot of revellers. And now she holds and feeds her new-born son. What does she think? Poet and artist have pictured her even then contemplating his path from birth to death. Journeys are in her mind. She has just come through a journey from Nazareth that, if not exactly a sorrowful way, has been a testing and a trying path to tread. But now, as poet and artist have imagined it, her concern is not so much with her own path, but with his. W. H. Auden expresses this with rare simplicity in his poem, 'At the Manger Mary sings'.

> O shut your bright eye that mine must endanger
> With their watchfulness; protected by its shade
> Escape from my care: what can you discover
> From my tender look but how to be afraid?
> Love can but confirm the more it would deny.
> Close your bright eye.
>
> Sleep. What have you learned from the womb that
>   bore you
> But an anxiety your Father cannot feel?
> Sleep. What will the flesh that I gave do for you,
> Or my mother love, but tempt you from his will?
> Why was I chosen to teach his Son to weep?
> Little One, sleep.

Dream. In human dreams earth ascends to Heaven
Where no one need pray nor ever feel alone.
In your first few hours of life here, O have you
Chosen already what death must be your own?
How soon will you start on the Sorrowful Way?
Dream while you may.[1]

The pain of the mother of Christ is located not only in
that series of rebukes that begins when Jesus is twelve:

Why were you searching for me? Did you not know
that I must be in my Father's house? (Luke 2.49).

Woman, what concern is that to you and me? My hour
has not yet come (John 2.4).

Who is my mother, and who are my brothers?
Whoever does the will of my Father in heaven is my
brother and sister and mother (Matthew 12.48–49).

Nor is it located only in the scene at the foot of the cross.
Her sorrowful way has already begun the moment she
begins to consider his. It is a way she accepts. In the
obedience of her response to the angel at the annunciation
there was an acceptance. Whatever may come, 'Here am
I, the servant of the Lord; let it be with me according to
your word' (Luke 1.38).

So glory to Mary? No, honour to Mary, but glory to
God. Glory only to God because the Christmas story is
told simply in order that we may grasp something of the
pain and suffering of God himself. Mary, by her willing
response to God, simply accepts a share in God's design
and carries with him the pain and suffering that is in his
heart. For all the beauty of his poem, surely Auden puts
too easily on to the lips of Mary the question

What have you learned from the womb that bore you
But an anxiety your Father cannot feel?

The twentieth century has struggled afresh with an old tension in the Christian tradition, between the Hebrew Scriptures and their willingness to attribute to God passions or emotions that human beings feel and the world of Greek philosophy that believes that God is beyond such things, impassible. Through most of Christian history the latter view has prevailed, but it has been much under fire in recent times. Almost too easily the other view has seemed to take hold of the Church. For it has been tempting, in a world the other side of Auschwitz and Hiroshima, to speak too glibly of a God of tears and indeed to attribute too easily to the deity our own human passions and emotions. Auden stands aside from that – 'an anxiety your Father cannot feel'.

Yet we struggle to find language that is theologically appropriate to express our view that God is touched by the pain and travail of his creation, that he does not sit unmoved outside it all. 'Anxiety' is an odd word to use of God and Auden is probably right to say God has none of it. But has God no pain? Does he not carry the pain and the suffering of the world, a world that strayed from him, a world of war and rumour of war? May we perhaps speak of pain in the heart of God when people kill one another mindlessly or cruelly, or turn away from injustice, and of joy in the aching heart of God when the peace of Christ takes over, however tenuously, in the affairs of his world? In the midnight darkness of Christmas, we celebrate, however inadequately we express it, a God who shares our pain and our suffering, as well as our joy, like Mary and like her Son, so soon to start on the sorrowful way. Glory to God. *Gloria in excelsis Deo.*

Consider now her husband, the carpenter of Nazareth. As Scripture pictures it, reassured by the angel he remains faithful to his pledge to marry Mary, though she is with child. He finds shelter for her in Bethlehem, and later leads mother and child to safety when Herod in his fear and fury plots the child's death. With the rumour of a massacre in the planning, Joseph begins to walk his own sorrowful way, escaping with Mary and Jesus into Egypt, like another Joseph before him whose journey was beset with humiliation, danger and threat of death itself. Later still, as Christian devotion has imagined it, coming out of Egypt and returning to Nazareth, Jesus learns the carpenter's trade at the hands of Joseph. And so, in crib and card, we picture not a mother facing childbirth alone, but at her side the faithful reliable Joseph, solid as the wood he carves and planes.

So glory to Joseph? No, glory to God. Glory to God because the Christmas story is told simply in order that we may grasp something of the faithfulness and reliability of God himself. Joseph, by his trustworthy protection of the mother and her child, simply reflects the unalterable and unbreakable faithfulness of the God in whom he believes. Despite the sinfulness and faithlessness of the human race, God remains always faithful. In the Hebrew Scriptures never more so than when the people of Israel came out of Egypt and rebelled and reneged in the wilderness for forty years. But now never more so than in the faithfulness of Christ. Faithful when ignored, faithful when rejected, faithful when hated, faithful even on a cross. Is it fanciful to think it no coincidence that the faithful Joseph's trade is that of a carpenter, making and shaping from wood? For the faithfulness of God leads him to be placed like a carved image on a tree, the wood of which has been shaped to be a cross. That is the total reliability of God. Joseph is the agent of it. So glory to God. *Gloria in excelsis Deo.*

Consider now the central figure of the drama, the Christ child himself. Picture the scene in crib and stable. Here is the King of kings, the Lord of lords, as a new-born child. It is a scene of unsurpassed simplicity and humility, marking the beginning of a life that will be like that every step of the way until the night before his death. Then he will kneel to wash his disciples' feet. Then he will let himself be handed over and will accept the death of the cross. On Christmas night shepherds kneel to the Christ child; yet what shines out of the crib is not *their* humility, in the stable on their knees, but *his*.

As Christmas gives way to Epiphany, there will come to the crib a scene so unexpected and extraordinary that it will seem to speak not only of humility but of a sort of foolishness. There is a seeming inappropriateness as into this simple scene in the crib march overdressed sages in gorgeous robes. Here come three Orient kings (though Scripture says nothing of their kingship), with crowns to prove it, armed with exotic gifts, and even, as it is sometimes portrayed, arriving by camel, to add to the menagerie. Christian devotion has made this scene familiar to us and protects us from its element of pantomime.

But the divine irony is that God is not to be found in the gorgeous robes, but in the swaddling clothes. God's wisdom is not in these wise men from the east with their trust in the stars, but in the foolishness of the new-born baby. The kingship that is indeed hidden in that scene is found neither in the cruel Herod nor in the eastern sages, but in the helpless one in the manger. The ultimate gift is not in the hands of the distinguished astrologers, but the child is himself the gift of God for wise and foolish alike. Here is the foolishness of God. It is not located only on the cross. It is here in the crib hidden in this implausible scene.

The magi withdraw, away again on their journey. It ought to have been a road of rejoicing, but maybe even this journey back home was a perplexing, sorrowful way, and not only because they heard that innocents had been massacred. T. S. Eliot's wise man tried to articulate it in 'The Journey of the Magi':

All this was a long time ago, I remember,
And I would do it again, but set down
This set down
This: were we led all that way for
Birth or Death? There was a Birth, certainly,
We had evidence and no doubt. I had seen birth and
    death,
But had thought they were different; this Birth was
Hard and bitter agony for us, like Death, our death.
We returned to our places, these Kingdoms,
But no longer at ease here, in the old dispensation,
With an alien people clutching their gods.
I should be glad of another death.[2]

It was the end of their world, 'the old dispensation', the old testament. There was pain and sorrow as something new was brought to birth. Yet the new thing that came to birth carried its own foreshadowing of death. Simeon (there was a wise man indeed) in the Temple when the child was presented saw it also: birth and death inextricably joined, and the glory in the joining. Christian piety has imagined at least one of the wise men from the east at least half perceiving it too when he brought his gift of myrrh:

> Myrrh is mine: its bitter perfume
> breathes a life of gathering gloom;
> sorrowing, sighing, bleeding, dying,
> sealed in a stone-cold tomb.[3]

So, surely, glory to Jesus? Yes, certainly, glory to Jesus, but only within the mystery of the Trinity that says more fundamentally: glory to God. Remember the song of the angels: Glory to God. For the heart of what the Church celebrates on Christmas night is not that Jesus was born, like any other human being, but that God was in Christ. It is the humility of God himself, who lays aside his divine nature to enter into the experience of our human life, with its joys and failures, tragedies and triumphs. It is the foolishness of God himself, upsetting our expectations and ushering in an order that is new and utterly surprising. It is God who is with us. That is what the Christmas story is trying to tell, that it is God who is among us. It is God who leaves the highest heaven to make his home among us. Glory to God for humility and foolishness unsurpassed.

Glory to God, for his pain, for his aching heart.
Glory to God for his reliability even to the wood of the cross.
Glory to God for humility and foolishness unsurpassed.
Gloria Deo, Gloria Deo, Gloria in excelsis Deo.

3

HOW LONG THEY HAD WAITED

Candlemas

They stand there, old Simeon and ancient Anna, full of years, of patient longing and of wisdom, a sense of expectation deep within them, for the Holy Spirit has prompted them once again. With the psalmist, they could say 'We have waited, O Lord, for thy loving kindness in the midst of thy temple' (Psalm 48.8 *Book of Common Prayer*). Yes, how long had they waited.

And now in this moment there is the promise of fulfilment. The young girl and her husband, with the pair of turtledoves, and with the baby forty days old, enter the Temple, overawed by its splendour, but eager to fulfil the law of the Lord.

It is only Luke who tells the story (2.22–40), the Presentation of Christ in the Temple on the fortieth day from his birth, and, though the child Jesus is at the centre of the story, it is the two couples who command attention. There are Mary and Joseph certainly, but even more there are the two old faithful ones, Simeon and Anna. Simeon, whom Luke tells us was 'righteous and devout, looking forward to the consolation of Israel, the Holy Spirit resting on him', guided by the Spirit came into the Temple and took the child into his arms and praised God in that song of ecstasy we have come to call *Nunc Dimittis*. Anna, a widow of eighty-four, who never left

the Temple but worshipped there with fasting and prayer
night and day, 'began to praise God and to speak about
the child to all who were looking for the redemption of
Jerusalem'.

It is their moment, not the young couple's moment so
much; it is their moment for Simeon and Anna. With
echoes of the prophet Malachi, they could say 'the Lord
whom you seek has suddenly come to his temple'
(Malachi 3.1). It is a moment of clarity, looking in two
directions, a moment rich in memory, a moment rich in
prophecy.

Memory: steeped as they are in their Jewish faith and
culture, they can recall, they can remember. It is not their
personal history, of course, but the history of their people,
the history of Israel, and the Temple in which they stand
is the symbol of it. They can remember the young woman
Hannah coming to the shrine at Shiloh, weeping,
distressed beyond words because she had no child. They
can remember her son, Samuel, presented to the Lord,
hearing his call and going to Eli who taught him to say,
'Speak, Lord, for your servant is listening' (1 Samuel 3.9).
They can remember Solomon building his Temple and
praying at its dedication, 'Hear the plea of your servant
and of your people Israel when they pray towards this
place; O hear in heaven your dwelling place; heed and
forgive' (1 Kings 8.30). They can remember invading
armies, destruction, exile, the Temple and the holy city in
ruins. They can remember restoration too. With the
prophet Haggai, they can say 'The latter splendour of this
house shall be greater than the former, and in this place I
will give prosperity, says the Lord of hosts' (Haggai 2.9).

Within the long deep memories of their people, they
can go back before shrines and temples and houses where
God dwells, to the beginnings, to the patriarchs, to the
years in Egypt, to a land of alien gods, and then to the

mighty workings of Yahweh – rescue, escape, liberation, salvation, God in a tent, and then the promised land.

Yet now again, they stand in the Temple, reflecting on their present circumstance, with Roman emperor and occupying forces, a kind of slavery, the land overrun by pagans, with their alien gods, and the glory gone from Israel.

They are rich in memory, but rich in prophecy too. As in the days of the prophet Joel:

> Your sons and daughters shall prophesy,
> your old men shall dream dreams,
> and your young men shall see visions.
> In those days, I will pour out my Spirit (2.28–29).

Anna, faithful daughter of Israel, prophesy! Simeon, old man of Israel, filled with the Holy Spirit, dream aloud your dreams! Here are prophetic eyes that in this tiny baby brought into the Temple see the salvation that God has prepared for all the nations to see; these pagans, with their alien gods, drawn into light, light to lighten the Gentiles, and once again the glory of Israel.

Yet if these holy ancient ones can see glory and salvation, what sort of glory can it be and what sort of salvation? For Israel's story is not of the Temple restored. It is of the siege of Jerusalem. It is of the destruction of the Temple. It is of the dispersion throughout the Gentile world. If not in their lifetime, then not very long after, before even the Christian Scriptures began to emerge, all this came to pass. Israel's story, as it continues, is of persecution, of racial intolerance, of faith set against faith, Christian against Jew in almost every country in Christendom, the new Israel of Christ set against the old Israel of Abraham. It is of Belsen and of Auschwitz. Yes, there will be fallings and risings, there will be rejection. Yes, young mother of Israel, a sword will pierce your soul.

Can that really be glory? And where in that lies any hope of salvation?

The Holy Spirit was upon them. It was the same Spirit who had overshadowed Mary when her Son 'was conceived by the Holy Ghost'.[1] It was the same Spirit who later would descend upon the young man coming for baptism in the River Jordan. It was the same Spirit who would empower the Church at Pentecost. That Spirit reveals to Simeon and Anna that here in this baby, forty days old, is both the glory and the source of salvation. From this baby, 'weak and helpless child of lowly Hebrew maid' as William Walsham How described him,[2] a light will shine out with glory and salvation.

And so they stand, on the day the Church calls the Presentation of Christ, or the Purification of Mary, or Candlemas. They stand with all that collective memory of Israel and all that half-perception of what is to be, and find hopes and fears and longings focus in that moment and meet in that child.

Like them (not altogether like them, of course, but in part like them), Christian people stand at Candlemas, looking back and looking forward, a day when past and future meet, and images come together to make a picture, satisfactory, complete and whole. They look back, in a sense to those far off days of Simeon and Anna, but in another sense only for forty days.

Back just to Christmas, back to the baby, weak and helpless, and to the crib, to a birth that, in the language of faith, spells love unsurpassed and the vulnerability of God. And then they look back to three images that belong to Epiphany, superimposed, so to speak, on the scene in the crib, but all expressions of the light and the glory and the hope of salvation promised in that new-born child.

They look back to the sight of three kings from lands afar, rich and wise, brought to their knees in face of God's poverty and foolishness in the child of Bethlehem. They look back to a picture of the young man come for baptism at the Jordan, with a glimpse of glory beamed from heaven, but still a vulnerability that drives him into the desert. They look back to the strange story of a wedding party, with too much drinking, too little drink, and a rebuke for the mother of the Lord; an earthy little tale that nevertheless has a hint of the new wine of the kingdom, a sense of wonder and the promise of glory.

In this mix of the ordinary and extraordinary, where humdrum life with feet on the earth is momentarily interrupted by shafts of light from heaven, they can see God showing something of his nature. The baby, the sign of God's love, humility and weakness, is growing to manhood, and in manhood he is still the sign of divine nature; loving, humble, vulnerable still. Until, at Candlemas, they are brought back for the last time for a final small glimpse of the baby. Forty days on, back to the baby, lest, in the picture of the man, the eternal message of God's love, humility and weakness should be obscured.

But Christian people have also found in Candlemas a foretelling and a direction in which to turn. For Candlemas lets them say farewell to Christmas and Epiphany, putting the crib away for another year, and points them, through a brief period in no man's land, to Lent and, in the distance at first, to a cross. At Candlemas Christians carry candles. They are echoing old Simeon's words: 'a light to lighten the nations'. They do not simply hold them. They walk with them in procession, through the Temple, so to speak. They will not walk together again like this until Palm Sunday. There will be no candle in their hands then, but palm, perhaps shaped into a cross. Through Lent to Holy Week, to the story of the sign rejected, denied, deserted, with Simeon's words coming back to them with poignancy:

This child is destined for the falling and the rising of many in Israel, and to be a sign that will be opposed so that the inner thoughts of many will be revealed – and a sword will pierce your own soul too.

Yes, there were two swords in the Garden of Gethsemane and Jesus said it was enough.

Jesus said to them, 'When I sent you out without a purse, bag, or sandals, did you lack anything?' They said, 'No, not a thing.' He said to them, 'But now, the one who has a purse must take it, and likewise a bag. And the one who has no sword must sell his cloak and buy one. For I tell you, this scripture must be fulfilled in me, "And he was counted among the lawless"; and indeed what is written about me is being fulfilled.' They said, 'Lord, look, here are two swords.' He replied, 'It is enough' (Luke 22.35–38).

Later from the cross he said it was finished, as the mother stood there with the broken heart. The body hung there, stripped, naked and humiliated, that the inner thoughts of many might be laid bare.

The candle the Christian holds at Candlemas is carried in procession to the font, where it is extinguished. 'Here we now stand near the place of baptism,' says the liturgy.

Help us, who are marked with the cross,
to share the Lord's death and resurrection.
Here we turn from Christ's birth to his passion.
Help us, for whom Lent is near,
to enter deeply into the mystery of Easter.[3]

The next time the Christian will carry a lighted candle will be at the liturgy of Easter. Into the Temple, so to speak, will come a great light, the light of the paschal candle, a light to lighten the pagans, glory for Israel. 'The light of Christ!' the deacon will sing. 'Alleluia! Christ is risen!' the Church will proclaim.[4]

Yes, the future that old Simeon and Anna saw meant siege, destruction, dispersion, intolerance, persecution, concentration camp, darkness, sword. But, taking the child into his arms, Simeon blessed God because he saw salvation, and Anna praised God and looked forward to the deliverance of Jerusalem. Did they perhaps see in the baby the man on the cross, still the sign of love and humility and weakness, still the sign of God? Did they see in that the strange mystery of glory and salvation the Church of Christ has seen? Did they see, when there had been darkness over the whole land, light, light for Israel, light for the world, flow out from an empty tomb? And did they see in the young baby brought into the Temple a sign of the resurrection body and the new life that shall encompass all things?

'Destroy this temple and in three days I will raise it up.' 'This temple has been under construction for forty-six years, and will you raise it up in three days?' But he was speaking of the temple of his body (John 2.20–21).

4

NO ORDINARY TIME

Before Lent

There is a kind of 'no man's land' between Candlemas and Lent, a short neutral season when the liturgical colour is green, a period technically called 'ordinary time'. The Christian year, with its cycles and seasons, is a great joy. Life would be drab if it were always ordinary time with no feasts and fasts. How exhausting it would be if we had the rigours of Lent for fifty-two weeks of the year. Yet perpetual Christmas or Easter would be almost as unbearable. It is the variety, the high points and the low, the joy and the restraint, the special and the ordinary, that make the Christian year such a delight.

But in some ways the Christian year is all too neat. Christians cannot only have a faith in the incarnation for forty days from Christmas to Candlemas. They cannot only look at their sinfulness and God's forgiveness for the forty days of Lent. They cannot survey the wondrous cross and be full of humble thankful praise only on Good Friday. They cannot live by faith in Jesus Christ risen from the dead just for fifty days from Easter to Pentecost. They cannot reflect on the power of the Holy Spirit only on Whitsunday. For the reality is that all the great Christian mysteries, the deep truths of our faith that we celebrate through the year, come at us at once, so to speak, and we need each one of them as part of our faith and living every day. Somehow we have to carry Christmas, Holy Week, Easter, Pentecost and All Saintstide, to name but five, with us through the year. The Christian calendar allows us to bring them to the fore in turn, so to speak, to give them a higher profile and to reflect on them and celebrate them the more. But they have to be truths that go deep within us all the time.

This is where the Eucharist comes in, for in a quite remarkable way it celebrates within the space of a few minutes all those truths, those Christian mysteries, that are so carefully unpacked during the year. Among the host of reasons why the Eucharist is a means of grace for the Christian, here is a particularly attractive and effective one.

The most striking example is, of course, at Christmas, when people flock to the Midnight Mass or come next morning, to celebrate the birth of Jesus Christ, and still what the Church offers them is the Eucharist, which in its great central prayer dwells principally on the night before Jesus died, on his death on the cross, and on his resurrection. We celebrate his birth by celebrating his death. T. S. Eliot's wise man would have understood that, just as Eliot's Thomas Becket did in *Murder in the Cathedral*. 'For whenever Mass is said,' the archbishop reminds his hearers in his Christmas sermon,

> we re-enact the Passion and Death of Our Lord; and on this Christmas Day we do this in celebration of his Birth. So that at the same moment we rejoice in His coming for the salvation of men, and offer again to God His Body and Blood in sacrifice, oblation and satisfaction for the sins of the whole world. It was in this same night that has just passed, that a multitude of the heavenly host appeared before the shepherds at Bethlehem, saying 'Glory to God in the highest, and on

earth peace to men of goodwill'; at this same time of all the year that we celebrate at once the Birth of Our Lord and His Passion and Death upon the Cross. Beloved, as the World sees, this is to behave in a strange fashion. For who in the world will both mourn and rejoice at once and for the same reason? For either joy will be overborne by mourning, or mourning will be cast out by joy; so it is only in these our Christian mysteries that we can rejoice and mourn at once for the same reason.[1]

It is a recognition that all Christian truths have to be held together and that, in the end, the faith cannot be divided up into convenient sized packages. Not just at Christmas, but every day, the Eucharist celebrates the birth of Christ. For every time Christians meet around the altar they act out again, in a small way, the miracle at Bethlehem. For just as, in that night, God sent his Son to be visible, touchable, just as in that night people could say 'Emmanuel' – God is with us – so in every Eucharist, in response to the Church's prayer, God sends his Son. Christ is present in the Christian congregation, his body today. Christ is present in the Scriptures, in which his voice is heard, present, visible, tangible. Christ is present in the bread and wine over which thanks is given, the bread and wine that, by God's grace, become for the Church the body and blood of Christ. In every Eucharist the Church can say 'Emmanuel' – God is with us. Sometimes in the Eucharist we say 'The Lord is here'. Yes, God is with us. Every Eucharist is a little Christmas, even in ordinary time, or even in Lent.

The Eucharist celebrates the death of Christ. Perhaps that needs no saying, for, if anything, the Church has tended to affirm that truth (though then to be locked in arguments about the relationship of cross and Eucharist) at the expense of all the other truths about the Eucharist. For every time we meet around the altar and eat the bread and drink the cup we 'proclaim the Lord's death until he comes', as Paul puts when writing about the Lord's Supper to the Christians at Corinth (1 Corinthians 11.26). We cannot, in the Eucharist or anywhere else, repeat the Lord's sacrifice upon the cross at Calvary. That was an event in time that needs no repeating. But, as the Church celebrates the Eucharist, and recalls the Last Supper and the death of Christ, Christians are drawn very strongly into his sacrifice, and the cross dominates the celebration. The bread that we break – the very breaking is a reminder of how the Lamb of God was broken upon the cross – is a share in his body which was given up for us. The wine that we drink is a sharing in his blood which was shed for us. There cannot be a Eucharist where the cross is absent. Every Eucharist is a walking in the way of the cross, even in ordinary time, or even on Christmas Day.

The Eucharist celebrates the resurrection of the Lord. That ought not to need saying, but it does, for through the centuries, and especially in the Reformed tradition, the cross has sometimes dominated even to exclusion of its corollary in the resurrection. Yet Sunday is the normative day of the Eucharist precisely because it is the day of the resurrection, and the eucharistic celebration is an extension of the great liturgy of Easter night and morning, not only during the Great Fifty Days from Easter to Pentecost, but every day.

For every time we meet around the altar we rejoice that the Lord has been raised and that in our midst is a Risen Lord. 'You raised him from the dead and exalted him to your right hand on high,'[2] we say in the Eucharist, and 'we proclaim his mighty resurrection and glorious ascension'.[3] And, when we come to the altar, though it is the body and blood of the one who died that we are given, yet it is also the body and blood of one whom death could not hold. It is the body and blood of the one whom we now know present and alive in the giving of thanks, the breaking and the sharing. Our experience is like that of the two disciples whose sorrowful way to Emmaus on the first Easter evening gave way to an encounter of joy when they recognized the Lord in the breaking of bread and rushed back to Jerusalem to share the news that the Lord was risen. You cannot have a Eucharist without the resurrection. Every celebration of it is a little Easter, even in ordinary time, even on the Sundays of Lent.

The Eucharist celebrates the gift of the Holy Spirit. Not just on the feast of Pentecost, but every day. For every time we meet around the altar we look up to heaven and ask God to send the Holy Spirit both upon the bread and the wine to make them for us Christ's body, and also upon us, as on those disciples in the Upper Room at Pentecost – the *epiclesis* the scholars call it; it simply means the prayer for the Spirit to be poured out. In some eucharistic prayers it is clear, explicit and inescapable. The Church of England's Third Eucharistic Prayer of Holy Communion Rite A expresses it thus:

> Grant that, by the power of your Holy Spirit,
> and according to your holy will,
> these your gifts of bread and wine
> may be unto us the body and blood of our Lord Jesus
>   Christ.[4]

> Send the Holy Spirit on your people
> and gather into one in your kingdom
> all who share this one bread and one cup.[5]

In other rites it is more hidden. But, explicitly or implicitly, in every Eucharist the worshipping community

29

asks the Father to send the Spirit and to renew within the Church the gifts of Pentecost and within the individual Christian the gifts first given in baptism. 'Send the Holy Spirit upon them to bring them to new birth in the family of your Church,'[6] the community has prayed over those who come to baptism, and now here in the Eucharist the Christian seeks a renewal of the gifts of the Spirit. In baptism we are drawn into the life of the Spirit and in the Eucharist sustained within that same life of the Spirit. For the coming of the Spirit is never so much a once-for-all event, whether at Pentecost or at baptism, but a sign of what God is always doing for those whose hearts are open – pouring in the Spirit, confirming the Spirit, renewing the Spirit, inspiring. You cannot have a Eucharist except by the power of the Holy Spirit, even in ordinary time, even in Epiphany. Least of all in Epiphany with its story of the Father sending the Spirit upon the Son in the waters of baptism at the Jordan River.

The Eucharist also celebrates the life of heaven, not just on Trinity Sunday or at All Saintstide, but every day. For every time we meet around the altar we do an essentially trinitarian thing that reflects that divine action in the Jordan. There the Father sends the Spirit upon the Son. Here, in the Eucharist, the Church asks the Father to pour down the Spirit that we may know the Son and receive his life into us once again. We enter the mystery of the Trinity and, like Abraham in Genesis 18, hover on the edge of a heavenly feast or, as the Rublev icon depicts it, find ourselves drawn within it. Rublev seats the three angelic figures, who, as in the story, seem at one moment to be messengers and at the next God himself, as if sharing a meal, but with a welcoming space for a companion to join the feast. We are bidden to enter the mystery of the Trinity itself.

'Holy Communion' we call it and, although that is

above all communion with God, communion with the Trinity, it is set within a wider context of a communion of saints. The Church on earth joins its prayers and praises with the whole company of heaven – angels and archangels, saints and martyrs, faithful people of every age. We pray for our dead (not, as some mistakenly imagine, to alter their eternal destiny, but simply to express our affection and gratitude for them within the communion of saints), and pray with our dead, and know the great company of the departed to be close to us, as we recall the death and resurrection of the Lord which is their salvation, as it will, we trust, be ours. May 'we, in the company of all the saints praise and glorify you for ever,'[7] we sometimes pray, and 'rejoicing in the fellowship of your saints we commend ourselves ... to your unfailing love'.[8] We need not only feel close to the departed in the dark days of November, when All Souls' Day comes round again, or with the saints each on their special day, but at every Eucharist know ourselves surrounded by a great cloud of witnesses, praising, praying, encouraging, loving. You cannot have an earthbound Eucharist, always you are being joined to heaven. Always you have an eye to the future. For, just as the Eucharist looks back to the Last Supper and also celebrates the reality of the here and now in the presence of the Risen Lord among his people, so also it looks to the 'marriage supper of the Lamb', as the Book of Revelation puts it (19.9). Every Eucharist is a daring anticipation of the feast of heaven. Every Eucharist has an element of Trinity Sunday to it, and a hint of All Saintstide too, even in ordinary time, even in February with hardly a saint's day in sight.

What a remarkable means of grace this sacrament is, renewing within us every time we share in it the great Christian mysteries of Christ's birth, death, resurrection, the gift of the Spirit, the experience of heaven. Christmas,

Holy Week, Easter, Pentecost, Trinity and All Saintstide all rolled into one. It is a marvellous, as well as rather unexpected, part of divine providence that what started as a simple supper, the night before Jesus died, has become such a vehicle of grace.

In the end perhaps there is never quite a 'no man's land' in the Christian year, no such thing, at one important level, as 'ordinary time'. At least there is never an empty time, with no point or purpose. Green, the colour for the weeks the calendar calls ordinary time (these weeks before Lent and then many more once Trinity Sunday is over) is the colour of growth, and what these periods give us is space to apply the great Christian mysteries that we celebrate in the seasons to our own lives. In a sense the spotlight moves from Jesus to ourselves, though only so that we can become more Christ-like. They are times to assimilate the truths that the feasts and seasons proclaim and to grapple with how these truths can affect us, change us, deepen us, help us grow. Green for growth – not neutral time, but growing time.

But this assimilating and grappling needs to be centred on the Eucharist. For the Eucharist is not only a staging post, a place of refreshment on the Christian journey, but also in itself a kind of microcosm of pilgrimage. Through its shape and dynamic and the way it handles the great Christian mysteries in a celebration not often more than an hour in length it brings us back to the way of discipleship and moves us along the path. Reliably, week by week, it speaks to us of the birth and the death and the resurrection of the Lord, of the gift of the Spirit and of the life of heaven. It is both refreshment for the journey and also a journey in itself.

5

STEADFASTLY TOWARDS JERUSALEM

The Sunday next before Lent

Six days later, Jesus took with him Peter and James and John, and led them up a high mountain apart, by themselves. And he was transfigured before them, and his clothes became dazzling white, such as no fuller on earth could bleach them (Mark 9.1–3).

The story of the transfiguration is a compelling tale. The mountain, Moses and Elijah, putting us in mind of law and prophets, the dazzling white, the cloud, the voice from heaven, the disciples almost lost for words – all conspire to give us one of those rare glimpses of divine glory. At the heart of the divine glory is the man, Jesus, whom Peter at Caesarea Philippi has just declared to be the Christ.

But why does the Church give us this story of the transfiguration on the Sunday next before Lent? The transfiguration often feels like an Easter event. It seems to half belong at least with those resurrection appearances where Jesus comes and goes, and belongs to the disciples but not quite, is a man in a body, but not in quite the way that he was. Transfiguration and ascension seem only a fraction apart. Here is a glimpse of the Beloved, the one made glorious. Indeed scholars will tell us that they think perhaps that is where the story did begin, a kind of resurrection appearance on a mountain. Be that as it may, Mark, followed by Luke and Matthew, saw it very differently. For Mark it belongs at a key moment in the ministry of Jesus and signals a fundamental shift in his self-understanding and in his fulfilment of his vocation. And if you had to find a time in the Christian year that could catch the mood of that moment and that shift it would be in that brief period between Epiphany and Lent.

For the season of Epiphany, coming to an end at Candlemas, has given us one by one glimpses of glory – signs, revelations, of the truth about Jesus. God had hidden himself in the baby of Bethlehem in such a way that only angels and humble folk with whom they shared the secret had even a clue of the truth. But, bit by bit, the truth came out. Here in this baby turned youth, turned full-grown man, the glory of God was shining. Some of them saw it when three wise men made their long journey following a star. Others knew it when the young man came to the Jordan and the Spirit descended like a dove and the voice spoke from heaven. They knew it when, in response to a foolish call, men abandoned the security of work and of family, to follow. They knew it when a fresh supply of wine at a wedding seemed to be the new wine of the kingdom. All these were epiphanies, moments of disclosure of the glory of God in the face of Jesus, whom they were beginning to call Christ.

For Mark, selective in the stories he tells, it is the baptism of the Lord that is the beginning of the sequence of disclosure. No magi in Bethlehem and no wedding at Cana for him. The beginning is the baptism with its 'You are my Son, the Beloved: with you I am well pleased' (Mark 1.1–11).

The ministry of Jesus emerges from that baptism and from the wilderness experience in which it is thought through. It is the ministry of a Jesus who rides high. There is the Jesus of a sort of bubbling thankful prayer, 'Father, I thank you …' (e.g. Matthew 11.25) time and time again. There is the entertainer, with his delightful stories that make you sit up or leave you spellbound. There are those magnificent moments of healing or power or fellowship.

Who then is this, that even the wind and sea obey him? (Mark 4.41).

He has done everything well; he even makes the deaf to hear and the mute to speak (Mark 7.37).

There is the overwhelming pull of a charismatic personality, for only a few maybe, but real enough for those ready to respond. 'Follow me', and they leave all at that instant to follow him. 'Take up your cross', a sober frightening call, but even that seems attractive in the company of this spiritual giant.

And yet there is failure. Jesus of all men was misunderstood. Great crowds misunderstood him. He fed them in a desert place, and instead of learning a lesson about communion, they could think only in terms of power politics and respond by wanting to make him a king. His disciples misunderstood him. When he tried to share with them something of his destiny, of what awaited him at Jerusalem, they looked blank or tried to dissuade him. His own family misunderstood him. His brothers and sisters tried to silence him and the people of his home region took up stones to throw at him. His teachings were so unpalatable that many deserted him. Though great crowds did come out into lonely places, they went away, perhaps disappointed, perhaps uplifted, but, either way, fading back into the obscurity of their daily living.

And there is suffering too. There are those who go through life unaware of their failure. Not so with Jesus. A man of his sensitivity perceived it all and it hurt him.

When the Fourth Gospel says that 'Jesus wept' (John 11.35 AV) it is in response to the death of his friend Lazarus, but 'Jesus wept', for all the joy and the confidence, is as accurate a summary of his ministry as any verse in the Gospels. Sickness, death, blindness to truth, all bring tears to his eyes and suffering to his heart.

There is a sense of alternation in the ministry of Jesus. One moment Jesus is, so to speak, riding high. Next moment, he is in the depths. But then comes the transfiguration, and it is in the transfiguration that these two strands, success and failure, glory and defeat, sorrow and joy, come together in a remarkable fusion. And for Mark this story of the transfiguration is the climax of the sequence of disclosure that began with the Lord's baptism. Mark has little to say of glory after the transfiguration. Mark, with his broken, doubting Jesus on the cross and his little more than hint of resurrection, locates the glory here in the transfiguration, and the voice returns: 'This is my Son, the Beloved: listen to him' (Mark 9.7).

If we contextualize the story as Mark tells it (and indeed as Matthew and Luke do also) we are confirmed in our view that it engages with the contradictions of the ministry of Jesus. For all that it is about divine splendour, it is set in a rather different world and is part of the search for the relationship between suffering and glory. It emerges directly out of Simon Peter's affirmation at Caesarea Philippi – 'You are the Christ' (8.29 AV) – that leads into one of those predictions of the passion that Jesus makes. And, once the story of the transfiguration is told, it gives way immediately to the story of an encounter with evil in healing a boy possessed by demons, and then to more talk of the passion, to conversation about conflict, and then, at least as Luke tells us, to Jesus 'steadfastly setting his face to go to Jerusalem' (Luke 9.51).

Furthermore it is unlikely to be coincidence that the

next time we hear an affirmation of Jesus as God's Son, it comes not in a voice from heaven, but in the words of the Roman centurion at the foot of the cross, 'Truly this man was God's Son' (Mark 15.39). It needed the cross for the human race to receive the message and to speak on the earth the truth that until then had only been heard from heaven.

The transfiguration was important for the crowd, for the disciples on the mountain, and for Jesus himself. It is Mark alone who gives us an important detail about Jesus as he comes down the mountain – one that indicates the significance of the event for the crowd.

When the whole crowd saw him, they were immediately overcome with awe, and they ran forward to greet him (Mark 9.15).

It must have been that the experience of transfiguration was still there in his face, for they were overcome with awe. It brings to mind Paul's words to the Church at Corinth:

The God who said, 'Let light shine out of darkness' has shone in our hearts to give the light of the knowledge of the glory of God in the face of Jesus Christ (2 Corinthians 4.6).

Yet it was not an awe that held them back. It was a wonder that drew them near. 'They ran forward', Mark tells us. That drawing to himself that reached its culmination in the cross had begun. For the crowd it was wonder that the transfiguration instilled.

For the disciples, Peter and James and John, with him on the mountain, the meaning lay more in their trust being renewed. With Peter as their spokesman six days before Caesarea Philippi, they had articulated their faith: this Jesus was the Christ. They had put their trust in him when they had first obeyed his summons to follow him. That first obedience must have been by instinct, rather than rationality, but in time they could begin to put it into words: 'You are the Christ.' And here in the transfiguration was confirmation of that – in the cloud, in the glory, in the voice. 'Yes, this is my Son, the Beloved.'

Suddenly they saw Jesus through God's eyes. The one they saw in white, in shining glory, was the man who shared with them the heat of the day, the toil of walking long distances on stony roads, and the sleeping rough of those who had no homes. The Jesus of the transfiguration was the one they knew – hot, sweaty, tired, needy – and he was transformed into the exalted Lord. Perhaps for the first time, they were seeing Jesus, not through their own tired eyes, but through the eyes of God. And they saw him for what he really was and for what he would become. Seeing Jesus through God's eyes, they saw the reality. The transfiguration illuminated and revealed for them the truth.

But it was not only the truth of who Jesus was that was confirmed, but something else too. For they had no sooner recognized Jesus as the Christ than he began to speak to them of suffering and death. This had been the moment, at Caesarea Philippi, when he had sharpened up his call, so that they were now not only invited to follow him, but to deny themselves and to take up the cross. That was the way that they were to follow him. They were to lose their life in order to gain it. They had not taken to that challenge. They could make no sense of it. Yet the voice that spoke from heaven said 'Listen to him'. It was not only their faith in Jesus that was being confirmed, but his words to them. They must trust his words as much as they trusted his nature, for his words, however unpalatable, were also stamped with the divine.

For Jesus also the transfiguration involved, perhaps, a

renewal of trust, a confirmation that he had indeed spoken true. But for Jesus it was above all the sharpening of vocation. The baptism, with the voice from heaven, had driven Jesus instantly into a wilderness to confront the forces of evil, 'to be tempted of the devil' (Matthew 4.1) as the gospel writers put it, to clarify his vocation, and then to emerge into the itinerant ministry of proclaiming the kingdom in word and deed, going where the Spirit led, a criss-cross of paths hither and thither. The transfiguration was the key moment when that mode of ministry came quite suddenly to an end. This time, not down to the river, but up into the mountain – everything important was to be up from now onwards, up to Jerusalem, up to the cross; a climb had begun. And, just as at the baptism, there came the voice from heaven, the Father enveloping the Son, that the vocation might be clarified, sharpened.

Returning from the mountain, Jesus enters a new kind of wilderness where, though he is not physically alone, he is more and more isolated, and the few who follow are increasingly puzzled and afraid. Straight away there is another encounter with the forces of evil – the devil back again – in the boy possessed with a demon, seen off by Jesus as before. But now there is no itinerant ministry. The vocation is crystal clear, the single-mindedness razor sharp. His face, still shining, is set towards Jerusalem. Nothing matters now but to suffer and to die, and so to beat the evil one yet again. It is as sharp a vocation as there could be and it is from the transfiguration that it emerges.

For Christians, standing in that space between Epiphany and Lent, the meaning is clear. If they stand in a wilderness with Christ, it is not the wilderness he entered at the beginning of his ministry. That is just a passing thought at the beginning of Lent. No, they stand with him in a new wilderness that begins after the transfiguration. Their eyes are on Jerusalem, on Good Friday and on

Easter. For Lent is about keeping up with the Lord who has set his face steadfastly in one direction and strides out with single-mindedness. Those who want to follow, even though the call now is to deny oneself and to take up the cross in order to follow, can learn from the transfiguration to take three things. The first is the recovery of wonder, like the crowd seeing the face of the Lord. The second is the renewal of trust, like the disciples recognizing the truth in his words as well as in his nature. The third is the sharpening of vocation, like the Lord himself. In Lent the Church works away at the recovery of wonder, at the renewal of trust and at the sharpening of vocation, holding clearly in mind that fundamental Christian insight, that amazing epiphany, that the suffering and the glory are the two sides of the same coin.

There were hints of it in those earlier tales of wise men, of old Simeon and Anna, of the baptism that drove into the wilderness and to the contest with the devil; always the suffering and the glory entwined. Never more so than in the transfiguration, Mark would say. Yet John's Gospel (at odds with Mark) protests that it is never more so than in one final epiphany, one final sign, one to which we may nevertheless say that the transfiguration points. Never more so, John would say, than on the cross, where the glory and the suffering are truly one. For John the cross is the last in the sequence of disclosure.

With wonder recovered, with trust renewed and with vocation sharpened, the Christian plunges into Lent, with eyes fixed firmly on Jerusalem and on the cross. It will be uphill all the way.

6

BREAD INSTEAD OF ASHES

Ash Wednesday

It is always strangely moving on Ash Wednesday going along the lines of Christian people standing or kneeling at the altar to receive the imposition of ashes. 'Imposition of ashes' sounds very grand, but the reality is different. It is a powerful little moment of sheer simplicity, yet deep intensity. There are ancient furrowed brows on which the sign of the cross is made. There are the faces of the young, slightly embarrassed, lining up to be ashed for the first time perhaps. There are eyes that are tightly closed, eyes wide open, eyes full of pain, eyes with deep joy. There are those haunting words: 'Remember you are dust, and to dust you shall return.'[1]

The priest stretches his hands over the bowl of ashes and prays.

> God our Father,
> you create us from the dust of the earth:
> grant that these ashes may be for us
> a sign of our penitence
> and a symbol of our mortality;
> for it is by your grace alone
> that we receive eternal life
> in Jesus Christ our Saviour.

What are we to make of ash as a symbol of mortality? 'Remember that you are dust and to dust you shall return.' They are, at least at first, uncomfortable words that the minister says as the cross is traced in ash on each person. It seems a hard saying, a reminder that in the midst of life we are in death; and for many it conjures up a memory of a graveside and those haunting words: 'earth to earth, ashes to ashes, dust to dust'.[2]

'Remember that you are dust.' It is, first of all, an invitation to humility. It is easy for many of us to grow in our sense of self-importance, whether at work, or at church, or in organizations to which we belong, or even in our assessment of our place in our family. There is, of course, a strand of self-esteem that is necessary for our health and well-being, but equally there is a self-regard that can be an insidious sort of sin. 'Remember that you are dust' is a timely reminder, putting us gently in our place. It is not that we are insignificant. You cannot be insignificant when God loves you. You exist, you are, you have being, because God created you out of the dust of the ground. You are, you continue to be, because you are enfolded in God's love. To be reminded of one's mortality is, in the end, a positive, not a negative, thing, for it is to have one's relationship with God affirmed. Though I am but dust, I live, I move, I have my being, because God loves me. This is a wonderful truth. It may prickle the bubble of my self-importance, but it also affirms my eternal value in the eyes of God.

It reminds me also of my heavenly destiny. Yes, my body will return to the dust from which it came. Yet, because God loves me, I shall not perish with my flesh and bones, but will be lifted up to him who first loved me into life and will draw me into immortality. When that will be, I can never know, but Lent is always an invitation to be ready and prepared.

So in the dust, the ash, and in the stern words, 'Remember that you are dust, and to dust you shall return', Christian people, as they begin the season of Lent, are reminded of the need for humility, assured of God's love that gives them breath, and pointed towards the immortality he longs to give them.

The ashes are to be a sign of penitence also. As the ash is traced on the forehead, the minister says not only 'Remember that you are dust', but adds, 'Turn away from sin and be faithful to Christ'. This is not much different from the Lord's first proclamation when he comes into Galilee when John is baptizing: 'Repent and believe in the good news' (Mark 1.15). By penitence we mean a real self-knowledge – What am I really like? How do I look to God? What is the truth about me? It is a self-knowledge that leads into sorrow, for the truth about me hurts, and sorrow, spending very little time in guiltiness or pity, converts itself into resolution, a firm intention of amendment, another fresh start in God's generous world of new beginnings. The dust, the ash and the gracious call, 'Turn away from sin and be faithful to Christ', strengthens in each one of us the self-knowledge that leads to sorrow, and the sorrow that is translated into resolution.

So Christian people on Ash Wednesday accept the cross of ash traced on their forehead. It is not an extravagant public humiliation. The Hebrew Scriptures are full of folk sitting publicly in ashes, wearing sackcloth, covering their heads in dust. God is often portrayed seeing through it all, and dismissing it as worthless. And the gospel reading on Ash Wednesday itself warns against parading our prayer and fasting.

Whenever you fast, do not look dismal, like the hypocrites, for they disfigure their faces so as to show others that they are fasting. Truly I tell you, they have

43

their reward. But when you fast, put oil on your head and wash your face, so that your fasting may be seen not by others but by your Father who is in secret (Matthew 6.16–18).

No, what Christians do on Ash Wednesday is anything but extravagant, essentially restrained, hardly public in what it leaves on their forehead once the dust has settled. It is an acting out in gesture what lips, in words, and hearts, in silence, have been trying to express: a recognition of mortality, which is a sobering insight (but in the end an affirming one, for God's concern is with our eternal destiny), and an expression of penitence, which is the crucial first step in the path of amendment of life. In the end the cross of ash is for every aspect of our humanity – for heart and mind and soul. Yet there is an appropriateness that it is on the body that the ash is traced, not only because it is that body that will return to the dust, but also because, in the spiritual struggle, it is often the body that lets us down. There is a self-indulgence of the heart and mind, but it is a self-indulgence of the body, whether in greed or sloth or lust, that often undermines our highest resolutions. 'The spirit indeed is willing, but the flesh is weak' (Mark 14.38).

It is the sign of the cross that is marked on the forehead. It is not, of course, the first time that the cross has been traced there. For, when new Christians come to baptism, they are signed with the cross, the sign that inspires them to confess the faith of Christ crucified. The cross on Ash Wednesday is a reminder of our baptism. In the innocency of our childhood or in the ardour of adult commitment, we received in baptism God's grace for our Christian pilgrimage. That pilgrimage goes on being a struggle, so often an upward climb, but we are engaged in it still, thankful for that grace without which the struggling would have been long since lost. Symbolically, on Ash Wednesday, we put the cross back, in ash this time as we recognize our failure, but the cross nevertheless.

Yet the cross on our foreheads looks in another direction too; back to our baptism, but forward to Holy Week. Lent is never a static season, but one that builds and develops towards Palm Sunday and Good Friday, as Christians seek to take more seriously and understand more clearly not only what it means to be 'signed with the cross', but also to 'take up the cross'. If the whole of Christian discipleship is about identifying with Christ, getting inside his skin, Lent is the time when it needs to be worked at with particular resolution. There is a looking back to our baptism in water, but there is also the forward thrust to Calvary, to be baptized with the baptism with which he is baptized. That is the Lent vocation and the cross of ash brings both the looking back and the looking forward into one focus.

The looking forward is to Calvary, but, of course, it is also a looking beyond that to Easter. The Christian does not pretend through Lent that there is no light at the end of the tunnel. The Christian lives always in the power of the resurrection, even in a solemn season of penitence. On Ash Wednesday we may employ cold ash, rescued from a fire long dead, but in the liturgy of the Church at Easter we shall gather around a new fire, burning brightly, hot and red, giving warmth. From it we shall light the paschal candle, the sign of the risen Christ into whom the Father has breathed new life. If, as we contemplate our mortality and our sinfulness, we seem like the coldest ash left in the long-unattended grate, we need to remember that God has the will and the power to breathe new life into the least promising of embers, to kindle in the coldest heart the burning fire of love.

But it not only ash that is given on Ash Wednesday, but, as at every Eucharist, bread also. The psalmist saw them as opposites:

> I eat ash like bread
> and mingle tears with my drink,
> because of your indignation and anger,
> for you have lifted me up and thrown me aside
>   (Psalm 102.9).

But that is not the Christian understanding. God our Father does not give us ash when we ask for bread. We may not be worthy to receive even the crumbs from under his table, but his property, his character, is always to have mercy. And so, sinners as we are, he gives us bread. Not the bread of this world's physical hunger, for Lent reminds us that we do not live by bread alone, but the bread, the sustenance, of his holy word, the word 'that proceeds from the mouth of God', and the bread also of the Eucharist, 'bread of angels' who ministered to Christ through forty wilderness days. The Church gives us ash, a sign of reconciliation. God gives us bread, the banquet for those who have been reconciled, and he gives it again and again.

Elizabeth Jennings reflects in similar fashion on the ashes and the bread.

> What ashes and what sackcloth now?
> We more than eat our fill each day.
> Lent is upon us. Few think how
> To do some penance and still see
> Christ's agony.
>
> He is with us in the Bread
> That's consecrated everywhere,
> And still a few take on a need
> And show their sorrow in a prayer
> And so repair

Their own and others' faults. They feel
All of Christ's suffering is still
About and some try how to heal
And help his steps up on that hill
Where men could kill

God as man. This mystery
Wise men could never understand
But here and there in history
A seer comes to comprehend
A man-God's end.

O yes he died. The sky went black,
Christ's own disciples fled away
Like Peter who would mourn his lack.
Our world is black and still we slay
Our God each day.[3]

On Ash Wednesday we learn and take heart from the
ash, but also from the bread, and begin to walk again with
the cross once more traced upon our forehead and in our
soul. For the invitation as Lent begins is always this: to
come, in humility, penitence and confidence, and to turn
to the Lord, who wipes the dust from our brow, and
places on our lips and in our heart the bread of heaven,
and the wine to make us glad again.

7

FINDING THE TRUE CROSS

Lent

One of the delights of working in a great cathedral is that it has so many different spaces for worship, different spaces to suit different occasions, and a cluster of chapels, all of them unique, but all for the celebration of the Eucharist. Each of them has its own character and nearly all have their own works of art. In some it is a painting and, where it is a painting, it is often on the east wall behind the altar. Looking at the paintings will often be an aid to Christian devotion and people would do well to go into all those chapels and sit down and gaze for a while to let the painting speak. Whether you think that looking at the paintings during the liturgy is an aid to devotion or a distraction from it will depend on how focused on the words and actions of the service you believe one has to be. But it is well nigh impossible to avoid doing so in some of the chapels of Norwich Cathedral if you stand there as a priest at the altar at the celebration of the Eucharist, as I do several times a week. I can hardly avoid fixing my eyes on the medieval painting in front of me as I speak the words of the liturgy.

It was, when first I came here, a new experience. In every other place where I have worked regularly, whether ancient cathedral or more modern church, I had usually stood at the altar facing the people, as we can also do here at some of our altars. And I had never really thought much about what I did with my eyes, what I fixed them on. I now know clearly what I did, and what I do when I am presiding at a Eucharist where the priest can face the people, and to that I will return. But, arriving in Norwich, I found myself at altars that you could not stand behind. The painting occupied that space. You had to stand west of the altar, back to the congregation. Standing there, what was I to do with my eyes? I did not think about it. I did what seemed natural. I fixed them on the painting.

Imagine the priest in St Luke's Chapel, off the south presbytery aisle, with that lovely reredos, probably the greatest treasure of the cathedral, all of six hundred years old, given to the cathedral by Bishop Henry Despenser and leading nobles of Norfolk in gratitude for their victory over a peasants' revolt in 1381. There, in the central panel, is the figure of the crucified Christ. The priest stands at the altar and speaks the words

> He opened wide his arms for us on the cross;
> he put an end to death by dying for us …
> Take, eat; this is my body which is given for you …
> this is my blood of the new covenant,
> which is shed for you and for many for the
>   forgiveness of sins …
> Grant that by his merits and death,
> and through faith in his blood,
> we and all your Church may receive forgiveness of
>   our sins
> and all other benefits of his passion[1]

and he fixes his eyes, and, in the mystery of the holy Trinity, he speaks in the name of the people to the Father as he looks upon the Son. That never ceases to move me, that you can fix your eyes on Jesus, and find yourself speaking to the Father; and therein lies a truth worth working through. The priest speaks of the passion as he looks on the Crucified One, the man of sorrows, the lamb of God who carries the sins of the world.

It is the same in the Norman chapel of St Andrew in the north transept, with its lovely crucifixion painting, probably of the same date, around 1385, part of a medieval retable, and brought from the Church of St Michael at Plea. Here also the priest fixes his eyes on Jesus, as he calls to mind the passion of the Lord, speaking for the people as they offer the sacrifice of praise.

In the Chapel of St Saviour at the east end of the cathedral, it is a little different. The five panels here are similarly of the Norwich School of the late fourteenth and early fifteenth century. The crucifixion is among them, but the central panel is of the risen, ascending Christ. And that witnesses to something important, for in the Eucharist we celebrate a risen and living Lord, not a dead hero who met an ignominious end. We have to move on from the passion to the vanquishing of death and the new life of the resurrection. But still the Christ who stands victorious bears the wounds, the scars, and not only on his hands and feet, but in his face and in his eyes. You can stand at the altar in St Saviour's Chapel and fix your eyes on the risen Lord and see and feel the pain of the cross still.

But then, come with me, if you will, into the Jesus Chapel, the next one as we walk around the ambulatory. For me it is one of the magical places in the cathedral. Nevertheless it has presented me with a major problem. There behind the altar is the *Adoration of the Magi*, painted in 1480 by Martin Schwarz of Rothenburg, with all its marvellous hats and headgear, which make one wonder whether it was the gift of a milliners' guild. In the centre of the picture is Mary, the mother of the Lord, and on her knee a diminutive holy child. And here is my problem. I stand there, with my back to the congregation, with this attractive colourful picture before me; and where shall I let my eyes be drawn? On what shall I fix them? On Jesus? It ought to be on Jesus. But this little baby has not a hint of suffering in his body or on his face. He is all innocent contentment, playing with the magi's gifts as if they were childish toys. This Jesus has not started on the sorrowful way. I cannot see the Christ of the cross, or the cross of Christ, in him. The words I am saying just will not marry with the picture. And I stand there, disorientated, searching for something on which to focus, something that will ring true with what is being said and what is being done.

My eye moves down to a sort of clasp, a tiny detail of the clothes of the wise man kneeling there. My eye is drawn there simply because the clasp is like a little jewelled cross, and the words of the Eucharist require me to find a cross. Or my eye moves to what is really a jewellery casket, out of which the child is drawing gifts, but which is shaped almost like a chalice.

> In the same way, after supper
> he took the cup and gave you thanks;
> he gave it to them, saying,
> Drink this, all of you;
> this is my blood of the new covenant.[2]

Somehow I must find a symbol of the passion. And then to the face of the Virgin, impassive, with eyes out of which the life seems to have drained, a kind of serene sadness apparently out of keeping with the coming of the kings. Yes, her face will do. It is not Jesus. It is Mary, but her face will do, because there is puzzlement, and perplexity and pain in it, and that face accords with the words that are being said. You can fix your eyes on the mother, and speak words to the Father, and be drawn close to the Son in his passion.

But my eyes have still not found one image on which to remain fixed. They have found a cross in a clasp, a chalice in a jewellery box, the face of Christ in his mother. But then I look at all the other faces too. They may be the faces of the retinue of kings, but, if they are, they have something of the quality of those magi whom T. S. Eliot described, the ones who had seen birth and death and had thought they were different, but found this birth hard and bitter agony. There is puzzlement, perplexity, even pain, in so many of the faces. It is not just the wonder of the coming of the wise men to the infant Christ. There is wonder, certainly, but there is pain. Maybe it is not a pain that foresees the suffering of the Lord. Maybe it is simply the pain of life, the marks it leaves upon us. But in every face, including the dark-skinned black king who becomes a kind of Simon of Cyrene, the African who carried the cross, you can see Christ. More than in the baby they called Jesus, you can see the Christ, the crucified one, in those faces the artist has given us.

It has been a struggle to find the right focus for the eyes as the Eucharist is celebrated. But the struggle has been worth it, for in the end, in the absence of the crucifix, I have found the focus. I have found it not so much in the clasp turned cross, nor the jewellery box turned chalice, nor even in the sword-pierced face of the mother alone, but Christ in every face, his passion in everyone's eyes. I have found the true cross.

Now I can tell you what I had not realized before. I have never needed a focus, a picture, a crucifix, when standing at the altar for the celebration of the Eucharist facing the people. For there before me is the crucified one, not in a painting, but in the people. The picture that marries up with the words that speak of suffering, of offering, of sacrifice, of pain, is the community of Christian people. It is in their faces, in their eyes, in the lines of their forehead that Christ's passion is being worked out. In each of them as individuals, with their needs, their hopes, their disappointments, their anxieties, their longings, the passion is being worked out. And in the Church as a community, with its corporate needs, and hopes, and disappointments, and anxieties and longings, the passion is being worked out. If I want to look on Christ, on his body marked with its wounds, I need only look at the community gathered around the altar, for this is the body of Christ, marked with its wounds. For all the appeal of his painting, I need no medieval artist.

But there is another little twist. It happens only in the chapel of St Andrew. The painting of the crucified Christ is covered with glass. Sometimes you look at the picture and in it, just for a moment, you see yourself reflected. If you are the priest at the altar, in your vestments, addressing the Father while wanting to fix your eyes on the Son, in the mystery of the Trinity, it is momentarily unnerving to see yourself, superimposed, so to speak, on the cross of Christ. You are looking for Jesus, and you see yourself, because of the glass.

Sometimes it is easier to locate Christ's cross today in other people. But Christ's cross today must be in me, each one of us must say. Each one of us must look at the cross and see himself, herself. Christ's cross today must be in me, because I need to be open enough to let him in, so that his cross and passion may interact with my experience, and bring, with interaction, understanding, resolution and healing. And Christ's cross must be in me also because, although he can and does take my sins away, he invites me to carry with him the burden of the world, which every day, in one sense, crucifies him afresh. Yes, we must see Christ in one another, but we must not be too frightened sometimes to see him in ourselves, Christ with his cross of pain and healing.

I am glad to have found the true cross or, more precisely, to have found the true faces upon the cross. One of them is my own, as in a glass darkly. But there are many such faces every time Christian people gather around the altar. Hardly ever do we need an artist to show us the likeness of Christ's body on the cross.

8

MAKING CONNECTIONS

Holy Week

In Dorothy L. Sayers' play, *The Just Vengeance*, written in 1946, an airman, who has just died in battle, arrives at his native city (it happens to be Lichfield), and finds himself being welcomed by its citizens from the past centuries, and required to state his claim to citizenship.

Recorder What matters here is not so much what you did
As why you did it ... Can you recite your creed?

Airman I believe in God ...

Chorus (picking him up and carrying him along with it)
... the Father Almighty, Maker of heaven and earth.
And in Jesus Christ ...

Airman No! No! No! What made me start off like that?
I reacted automatically to the word 'creed' –
My personal creed is something totally different.

Recorder What is speaking in you is the voice of the city,

> The Church and household of Christ, your
> people and country
> From whom you derive. Did you think you
> were un-begotten?
> Unfranchised? With no community and no
> past?
> Out of the darkness of your unconscious
> memory
> The stones of the city are crying out. Go on.[1]

What is that saying? It is reminding you that, for all your individuality, for all your intensely personal experience, you are no isolated self. Your belief is part of a community of belief, your story is everybody's story. Palm Sunday ushers in the holiest week in the Christian year. When we tell the story of the passion, the death and resurrection of the Lord, we are expressing our belief in what happened to him. But, more than that, we are expressing our conviction that it has significance for us. We are declaring our recognition that his story turns out to be everyone's story, and that everyone's story turns out to be my own story too. We are proclaiming that the faith of the creed echoes something deep inside me about the depths of my being.

Let us go back for a moment to the Jewish people, the first to hear the word of God. Consider their annual commemoration of the Passover and the Exodus. When each year the festival time came round, the Jews relived that experience, not as the mere recalling of something significant that had happened to their ancestors long ago, but as an experience through which they themselves were going. So powerful was this for them that it was, in reality, the making present of a past event. But it was the making present of a past event in the knowledge that a past event is simply a pin-pointing in time of an eternal truth.

Or look at the Christian Eucharist. We talk of the Lord giving us his body and his blood and we recognize his presence in our midst. Again that is the making present of a past event, in the knowledge that a past event is a pin-pointing in time of an eternal truth. The key word in the Greek is *anamnesis*, which we translate as 'remembrance', but it cannot be said too often and too loudly that our idea of remembrance is much weaker than this exciting experience of the past drawn into the present.

We need to hold that idea – that the past is made present and is found to reflect an eternal truth – in mind for a moment, and consider a second slightly different thing. Think for a moment about the experience of Jesus in what we now call Holy Week. Call to mind all the emotions and events that gripped him, from his triumphant entry into Jerusalem until his ignominious end at Calvary. It is quite a catalogue: popularity, anger, exhilaration, fellowship, love, fear, betrayal, helplessness, isolation, pain, and death itself. Are these not the emotions and experiences of every person? And, in some small measure, is not much of this your experience too?

The past is made present and is found to reflect an eternal truth. The experience of Jesus is the experience of every person. We need to hold these two ideas in mind, and look at a third and last. It is the same truth from another angle.

There is a human need, that most will recognize, to share, to talk about, to recite over and over again, particular events and experiences that have made a mark upon us, events whether of sorrow or of joy. 'Do you remember the day we ...' Or 'I shall never forget the way I found him ...' We do it especially with death. We go over the details, often with those who know them already, because we are not simply conveying information, nor are we simply remembering, though the need to do that is strong. It is that the recitation, the repetition, brings clarity and insight. Talking about it, talking it through, brings reconciliation and acceptance. It is part of the process of wholeness and healing.

We can now put together these three related themes:

* The past is made present and is found to reflect eternal truth.
* The experience of Jesus is the experience of every person.
* The rehearsal of past events brings insight and healing.

Together they give the rationale of Holy Week. Like the Jew at the Passover, I hear how God acted, in Jesus long ago, but know it to be an account of how he acts in every person in every age, and know it to be how he acts in me today. Holy Week becomes this week. Jesus becomes me. And in that exercise I learn to understand myself, my lot, my destiny, God's role for me, God's care for me. As a human being I grow in my maturity.

Holy Week is not just a liturgical game. It is a powerful drama of the deepest realities about myself and about every person. It is more than liturgy, more even than theology. It is about the depths of my being. That is why the Church invites Christian people to enter as deeply and seriously as they can into the experience of Holy Week in preparation for the celebration of Easter. Holy Week is like a great symphony, with its several movements each with its distinctive mood. You can listen to one movement of a symphony and find it attractive. But, if you want to enter into what the composer is trying to convey, if you want to be gripped by the music and thrilled by it or touched by it, you need to hear it all.

So what are the movements of this symphony that the

Church plays through Holy Week? First is Palm Sunday morning, when the Church commemorates the Lord's entry into Jerusalem to accomplish his saving work by dying and rising again. A procession of palms is not only a reminder of what happened on that day, but is an act of praise to Christ the King who reigns and triumphs on the cross, and it expresses our own readiness to take up our cross and follow the crucified and risen Lord, as we go with him to the place of suffering and death. Though we walk into Jerusalem, so to speak, we also begin to walk the last stage of the sorrowful way.

The second movement is the liturgy of Maundy Thursday evening. Joyfully we gather to share in the supper of the Lord, gathered around the table as in the upper room. But not going to our homes until, the supper ended, we have entered into the experience of the agony in Gethsemane Garden, the darkness crowding in, the desertion of friends and the trial through the long hours of the night.

And so to the third movement, the liturgy of the cross on Good Friday, coming to that cross with Christ, sharing his love and his pain, and expressing that by sharing also the bread which is broken, and the wine that has been poured out, the body and blood of Christ, and bringing the sufferings of humanity to the Lamb who takes away the sins of the world. It is a slow movement of deep emotional complexity, yet with a confidence all its own.

But then the last great movement – Easter – with its mood of joyful irrepressible celebration and its crescendoes of praise. But that is a story for another day.

As a priest one sometimes has the privilege of ministering to a Christian man or woman near to death. It is always a moving experience and deeply humbling. Just occasionally that has been happening through the days of Holy Week, and I have found myself moving out of the liturgy to the hospital or to their home, and back into church, and so on. I remember once on Maundy Thursday after the Eucharist of the Last Supper, sharing in the watch in the church and then slipping out to keep another watch at the bedside of a dying man, and then returning to the church to rejoin the figures kneeling there in the darkness. Both in the church and at the bedside I had a clear sense of 'watching with Christ', each experience illuminating the other.

Or, to take another example, I will always remember coming out of the Good Friday Liturgy and driving to visit another dying man. In the preaching and the worship we had been exploring the words Jesus spoke from the cross with his dying breath. At the bedside I sat with the man who, full of drugs to ease his pain, could not find the words to speak as coherently to me as he wanted about his own death and about his funeral.

You cannot move from the liturgy to these 'real life' experiences without making connections, without seeing that in the experience of Christ is the experience of every person, and without seeing how a lifetime of trying to follow Christ in the way of the cross gives to those suffering and near to death resources that make them spiritually strong and able to face everything with a gentle, accepting faith.

Now that is the ultimate walking in the way of the cross. We walk it only once for ourselves, but more often with others whom we love. The dying man to whose bedside I drove that Good Friday afternoon was my own father. But I am not saying that we keep Holy Week simply to prepare us to be strong in the face of death. We keep Holy Week to make us open, sensitive and faithful in all the testing experiences of human life, to help us make connections in all of them.

That is why the president of the liturgy says on Palm Sunday morning

> Let us go with Christ in faith and love, so that, united with him in his sufferings, we may share his risen life.[2]

If something more than conventional piety encourages me to respond to that invitation, it is perhaps that, deep down, I know that, in some small measure, it is I who hang upon a cross and my story that is being told. In the retelling of it I receive insight and healing. It is indeed the cross of Christ that heals.

> Behold the Man.
> Behold, Lord, every Man, every Woman.
> Behold, my Father, me.

9

ARE YOU A KING?

Palm Sunday

Six days before the Passover Jesus came to Bethany, the home of Lazarus, whom he had raised from the dead. There they gave a dinner for him, Martha served, and Lazarus was one of those at the table with him. Mary took a pound of costly perfume made of pure nard, anointed Jesus' feet, and wiped them with her hair ...

The next day the great crowd that had come to the festival heard that Jesus was coming to Jerusalem. So they took branches of palm trees and went out to meet him, shouting, 'Hosanna! Blessed is the one who comes in the name of the Lord – the King of Israel' (John 12.1–3a, 12–13).

Those who witnessed the entry of Jesus into Jerusalem could not fail to remember the words of the prophet Zechariah. Indeed John quotes them: 'Look, your king is coming to you' (Zechariah 9.9). What kind of king is this who enters his city?

Later in the story, as John tells it, we hear how the Roman governor presented Jesus to the crowd with the ironic cry 'Here is your King' (John 19.14) and placed over the figure of the dying Christ upon the cross the description, 'Jesus Christ, the King of the Jews' (John 19.19). But, first, in the story of Palm Sunday and his entry into Jerusalem, we have a coronation and a coronation procession. 'Mary took a pound of costly ointment made of pure nard, anointed Jesus' feet, and wiped them with her hair' (John 12.3). Or, a little differently, as Matthew puts it, 'a woman came up to Jesus with an alabaster flask of very expensive ointment, and she poured it on his head' (Matthew 26.7). This is the kind of anointing associated with priests and kings. At the heart of the coronation ritual in Westminster Abbey, last seen at the coronation of Queen Elizabeth in 1953, the moment of supreme religious significance is the anointing of the sovereign. 'Be thy head anointed with holy oil,' says the archbishop.

> as kings, priests, and prophets were anointed, be thy breast anointed with holy oil, be thy hands anointed with holy oil. And as Solomon was anointed king by Zadok the priest and Nathan the prophet, so be thou anointed, blessed, and consecrated.[1]

Here, in the house at Bethany, something like this happens to Jesus. The significance is not lost on the disciples, for next day we find the newly anointed king riding into the holy city as the crowds acclaim 'Blessed is the one who comes in the name of the Lord – the King of Israel' (John 12.13).

Yet there was in the life of Jesus an ambivalence about kingship. When Jesus comes to John on the bank of the Jordan the voice had been heard and the Father had claimed him as his own. 'You are my Son, the Beloved' was what they heard from the cloud, and every Jew knew that, in the terms of the Hebrew Scriptures, these were the words of God to the king, to David's heir and descendant. The baptism is a first anointing, the recognition of the crown prince, who will eventually enter into his kingdom in the holy city. But this first time, by the

Jordan, there is no crowd and no triumphal procession. Rather, the young man flees, puzzled, perhaps afraid, into a desert place, there to think through the destiny that begins to dawn upon him. There is no easy acceptance of the role or title of a king. Later, when the great multitude has been fed with loaves and fishes, John tells us that Jesus 'realized that they were about to come and take him by force to make him a king and withdrew again to the mountain by himself' (John 6.15). Jesus shies away from the kingship that they offer. Nevertheless on Palm Sunday his acceptance seems total, for he finds a young donkey and sits upon it, knowing that the crowds will recall the words of Zechariah: 'Shout aloud, O daughter of Jerusalem! Lo, your king comes to you; triumphant and victorious is he, humble and riding on an ass' (Zechariah 9.9). It is a clear acceptance of the kingdom.

What has happened? What has changed? Why does he now accept what before he rejected? The answer lies perhaps in the exchange between Jesus and Pilate later in the week:

> Pilate entered the headquarters again, summoned Jesus, and asked him, 'Are you the King of the Jews?' Jesus answered, 'Do you ask this on your own, or did others tell you about me?' Pilate replied, 'I am not a Jew, am I? Your own nation and the chief priests have handed you over to me. What have you done?' Jesus answered, 'My kingdom is not from this world. If my kingdom were from this world, my followers would be fighting to keep me from being handed over to the Jews. But as it is, my kingdom is not from here' (John 18.33–36).

Jesus is a profoundly original thinker. Every term of address that he receives is accepted, but reinterpreted, almost, you could say, turned on its head.

'You are the Messiah.' 'Yes. But. If I am the Messiah, it is not the sort of messiah you envisage. Remember Caesarea Philippi. "You are the Christ, the son of the living God." Yes, but I must go to Jerusalem and suffer many things and be killed. Not your idea of a messiah, but a whole new view.'

'You are Master.' 'Yes. But. You call me Master and Lord, and rightly so, for that is what I am, but ...' (John 13.13 RSV). The story of the foot-washing belongs to later in Holy Week, but again it is the acceptance of the title, but the investing of it with new shades of meaning. The master who is the slave, the master who waits upon the servants.

'You are the Son of man.' 'Yes. But. But a whole new view of what it means to be authentically human.'

And now 'You are a King.' 'Yes. But.'

What sort of king is he who rides into the holy city on the first Palm Sunday? How is kingship remoulded in his creative hands? First, the king comes with humility. He chooses to ride on a beast of burden, a young ass rather than a war charger. Here is something new, a reinterpretation of kingship, with humility as its mark. Yet it is still as a leader that Jesus rides into the city. He has not abdicated his responsibility. He will lead into battle. He will not hang back or surround himself with bodyguards, or send others in to be struck down first. Furthermore he will, if necessary, wage war single-handed. He will take on the enemy champion in combat. The enemy champion is the devil and he will indeed take him on alone and win. The king will die for his people without thought to personal cost, and thus will blaze the trail into the freedom of the promised land for all his people. But the weapons are novel and the power a strange unpromising sort where strength seems to be weakness, and human standards have no meaning. Kingship is transformed. The cry 'Hosanna' is henceforth to be for a new kind of leader, one who comes in gentleness, in simplicity and even in weakness. There is no room in the kingdom of Christ for the sophisticated and the arrogant, the harsh and the strong.

We cannot know what thoughts and emotions were passing through the mind of Jesus as he rode into the city. He knew that his hour was coming and he understood at least in part what that must mean. He knew himself to be a king. He knew that a crown would be pressed upon him. But he knew that his kingdom was not of this world. Perhaps, being human, he responded with exhilaration and delight at the joyful festive reception that accompanied his arrival. But probably even then he knew the shallowness of human, worldly praise and hero-worship. Maybe he sat light to all the excitement and the fuss. Or maybe in the excitement of the crowd he perceived the return to tempt him again of that devil whom he had so summarily dismissed after his first anointing by the bank of the Jordan. 'When the devil had finished every test, he departed from him until an opportune time' (Luke 4.13 BCP).

There is a final twist to this theme of kingship as the New Testament presents it. The First Letter of Peter asserts that 'you are a chosen race, a royal priesthood, a holy nation, God's own people' (2.9). The Revelation to John speaks of the one who has loved us and freed us from our sins and 'who has made us to be a kingdom, priests serving his God and Father' (1.6). Kings and priests are we all. 'He hath exalted the humble and meek' (Luke 1.52). We are no longer slaves, servants, but now kings and priests, anointed as such by our baptism. But we have to keep in mind the pattern for Christian royalty: humble (the donkey not the horse), serving (not waited upon, but waiting at table and washing feet), unassuming, unpretentious, but going into battle, taking a lead, out in front when a battle needs to be fought, fighting, despite the world's strategists, from a position of weakness, willing to die a thousand deaths with the promised land in sight. That is to drink the cup that he has drunk and to be baptized with the baptism with which he is baptized.

Kingship is a difficult vocation and a demanding one. The ambivalence of the Bible about it is understandable. The reluctance with which Jesus assumes it is not to be wondered at. But in the end he accepted not only the anointing, in the house at Bethany, and the acclaim, along the road into the city, but the crown that was pressed upon him – the crown of thorns. And in the Christian life we live with the possibility that again and again that crown may be offered to us too.

Christina Rossetti puts these words on to the lips of the priest-king upon the cross in her poem, 'The Love of Christ that passeth knowledge':

> I bore with thee long weary days and nights,
> Through many pangs of heart, through many tears;
> I bore with thee, thy hardness, coldness, slights,
> For three-and-thirty years.
>
> I bore thee on my shoulders and rejoiced:
> Men only marked upon my shoulders borne
> Thy branding cross; and shouted hungry-voiced,
> Or wagged their heads in scorn.
>
> Thee did nails grave upon my hands, thy name
> Did thorns for frontlets stamp between mine eyes:
> I, Holy One, put on thy guilt and shame;
> I, God, Priest, Sacrifice.
>
> Nailed to the racking cross, than bed of down
> More dear, whereon to stretch myself and sleep:
> So did I win a kingdom – share my crown;
> a harvest – come and reap.[2]

10

BOWL AND FONT AND SPEAR

Maundy Thursday (1)

Image of the eternal Father,
Ruling all created things,
Holding distant worlds together,
Lord of glory, King of kings.

Stepping down from heavenly splendour,
Taking here the lowest seat;
By your humble birth among us
Washing your creation's feet.

By the towel, the bowl, the water,
By the thorns, the nails, the spear,
Lord have mercy, Christ have mercy:
Love unknown enfold us here.[1]

Edwin le Grice's poem was inspired as much by the *Song of Christ's Glory*, Paul's great hymn in the Letter to the Philippians, as by John's account of what happened in the Upper Room on Maundy Thursday night. It helps us to see in the action of Jesus washing his disciples' feet important clues to the character of God. For it is nothing less than something of the character of God himself that we ought to look for as we picture Jesus getting up from table, taking off his outer robe, tying a towel around himself, pouring water into a basin and beginning to wash his disciples' feet and to wipe them with the towel.

There is, first of all, a message in terms of humility. Paul in that great hymn in his Letter to the Philippians has spoken of it in these terms:

Let the same mind be in you that was in Christ Jesus,
who, though he was in the form of God,
did not regard equality with God
as something to be exploited,
but emptied himself,
taking the form of a slave,
being born in human likeness (2.5–7).

The humility of Christ lies in the truth of who he really is. It is not the humility of a man that is demonstrated in this story, but the nature of God that is revealed. Here we are given a reminder, as we enter into the passion of Christ, of the truth that Christmas first spelt out. The great God, the creator of heaven and earth, has taken on human shape and form and nature, as a weak and helpless baby. He who rules the constellations has made his home in a human body. Too easily we call that 'incarnation' and by giving it a name make manageable an almost incomprehensible truth. The very thought of it should bring us to our knees, as it did shepherds and kings alerted by angels and star. But here we discover, when the child has grown into a man, not that we are brought to our knees by this tremendous mystery, but that it is he, this God in Christ, who falls to his knees to wash the feet and wipe them with the towel.

The action speaks also of service. Although it is only John who tells the story of the washing of the disciples' feet, the other Gospels place on the lips of Jesus the same truth that he expresses in this powerful ritual. 'You know,' says the Jesus of Mark's Gospel,

that among the Gentiles those whom they recognize as rulers lord it over them, and their great ones are tyrants over them. But it is not so among you; but whoever wishes to be great among you must be your servant, and whoever wishes to be first among you must be slave of all. For the Son of Man came not to be served but to serve, and to give his life a ransom for many (Mark 10.42–45).

It is another stage in Jesus' revolution, his turning on its head of much conventional wisdom. Henceforth the mark of authority is to be service. The greatest in the kingdom will be the one who does the most menial task, the one who is willing to serve brothers and sisters in the most menial of stations.

But, for all the richness of their meaning within the context of this story, both these words – humility and service – seem inadequate to express what Jesus is doing and bids us do. Only a third word expresses strongly enough what is at stake. We have to read on in chapter 13 of John's Gospel, beyond the foot washing story, to find the clue, for it is when Judas has gone out that Jesus says 'I give you a new commandment, that you love one another, just as I have loved you' (John 13.34). And he adds for good measure that it is by this love for one another that everyone will know that we are his disciples. It is only 'love' that expresses strongly enough what is being shown to us here.

For it is love that best describes what Jesus does when he fetches bowl and water, jug and towel. It is not simply the humility of the God who is on his knees, nor the lesson in service of the master who behaves like a slave, but the love of one generous, warm, impulsive and affectionate in his loving. Jesus is not giving an object lesson in good relationships. Nor is he acting out a sort of parable. He is doing it because he wants to do it. He is doing it because the tired, hot, sweaty feet in need of washing are the feet that belong to his friends, his close companions, his adopted family. It is an act of love, generous, embarrassing, natural love. We must not imagine for a moment a solemn ecclesiastical ritual. This is a joyful act of self-giving. And Jesus adds to hammer home the point: 'By this will everyone know that you are my disciples, if you have love for one another' (John 13.35). People will know that there is something of Christ in you if there is a warmth, a joy, a natural affection, an impulsive generosity breaking out in all your human relationships.

Washing feet during the Eucharist of the Last Supper on Maundy Thursday evening is not always good theatre. It is down on the ground among the people, visually fairly hopeless, and to put it up on a stage would violate its message. However hard those who sanitize the liturgy try, it is never an aesthetically pleasing ritual – not many people have beautiful feet and trying to dry between somebody else's toes requires a sure touch. But you will not often find a priest who has knelt to wash the feet of parishioners on this day or a person who has had their feet washed in this way who has not been profoundly moved by it. It is essentially a relational ritual. Even in the context of the local church community, it is about humility and about service, but still it is chiefly about love. Love within the Christian community, especially the love of the priest for the people is an area of great sensitivity, fraught with danger, and there is a kind of professionalism in Christian ministry that urges detachment. People are wise to heed the warnings. Yet Maundy Thursday makes its own protest against our reticence. Get down on your knees, the story says, and love.

The hymn for the foot-washing, whether sung in cathedrals to the music of Maurice Duruflé or in parish churches to the music of Gregory Murray or in another contemporary form, is *Ubi caritas*, the key line of which is also known to many as a popular chant from Taizé. *Ubi caritas* was composed for the foot-washing in a Benedictine community in Reichenau about AD 800. Through the centuries in monasteries and churches it has formed a musical backdrop to this powerful bit of liturgy:

> God is love, and where true love is, God himself is there.

> Here in Christ, we gather, love of Christ our calling;
> Christ, our love, is with us, gladness be his greeting;
> Let us all revere and love him, God eternal:
> Loving him, let each love Christ in all his brothers.

> God is love, and where true love is, God himself is there.

> When we Christians gather, members of one Body,
> Let there be in us no discord, but one spirit;
> Banished now be anger, strife and every quarrel:
> Christ our God be present always here among us.

> God is love, and where true love is, God himself is there.[2]

Get down on your knees and love, for where true love is, God himself is there. But Simon Peter cannot cope. Back at Caesarea Philippi, it was Simon Peter who had recognized who this Jesus really was. How can the Messiah, the Christ, kneel at his feet and wash them? It cannot be right. It was Simon Peter who again and again had called Jesus 'Master'. How could the master turn into a slave? It cannot be right. It was Simon Peter, impetuous uncomplicated Peter, who was later to reassure his master and his Messiah that he loved him, and who was to be hurt that Jesus should ask him the third time, 'Simon, son of John, do you love me?' (John 21.16), who now cannot receive the Lord's expression of love for him. There is something of that in most of us. 'Yes, Lord,' we might say, with Peter, 'I am willing to love, to love you and to love my neighbour, but, Lord, don't love me too much, don't let my neighbour love me too much.'

> Simon Peter said to Jesus, 'You will never wash my feet.' Jesus answered, 'Unless I wash you, you have no share with me.' Simon Peter said to him, 'Lord, not my feet only but also my hands and my head!' Jesus said to him, 'One who has bathed does not need to wash, but is entirely clean' (John 13.8–10a).

The words of Jesus in reply to Peter are not straightforward. What he means, or so we must imagine, is that the one who has bathed in the water of baptism has no need to wash again, for he is entirely clean. This washing of the disciples' feet is indeed a sort of baptism. Three years before, when Jesus stood by the bank of the Jordan, he had been baptized at a point far below sea level, one of the lowest points on the earth, and that had seemed to represent the depth of his humility, his going down as low as humanity can go. And now, again, he goes down on his knees and, from the ground, he who is the Living Water washes the feet of his disciples that they may have a share in his destiny.

He comes to James and John, and perhaps they recall his penetrating question of a while before. Can they drink the cup that he will drink? Can they be baptized with the baptism with which he is baptized? He had told them they would indeed share his baptism. Here now is a kind of baptism with water, but ahead a baptism of blood in a martyr's death, and for Simon Peter too.

Bread and wine, and water too, are interwoven into the gospel story, and into the passion in particular, for baptism brings the Christian to share in the dying and rising of Christ, and the Eucharist constantly renews the Christian's commitment to live in the power of that mystery. Water in the Jordan, water in baptism, water in the upper room poured over disciples' feet, water mixed with wine in every Eucharist, and water, living water, flowing from the side of the lifeless Christ. 'One of the soldiers pierced his side with a spear, and at once blood and water came out' (John 19.34). As he washes their feet Jesus, perhaps, looks back to his baptism in the water of the Jordan and forward to the cup that he will drink and the baptism with which he is to be baptized on a hill outside the city where, in the parched noonday sun, he will cry 'I am thirsty' (John 19.28). And water will flow from the side the soldier will pierce with a spear.

For ultimately it is not in the upper room, but upon the hill top, that humility, service and love find their most compelling expression. For the humility of God, the sheer self-emptying and self-denial, is seen most clearly not in the washing of feet, nor even in the child lain in the manger, but in the man who hangs on the cross. Christian service reaches its climax, as Jesus himself had taught, when it leads to Calvary. 'For the Son of Man came not to be served, but to serve, and to give his life a ransom for many' (Mark 10.45). And love too had to lead to the cross. Only there could the full generosity of it be apprehended. Jesus knew that. 'No one has greater love than this, to lay down one's life for one's friends. You are my friends' (John 15.13).

> Love that gives, gives ever more,
> Gives with zeal, with eager hands,
> Spares not, keeps not, all outpours,
> Ventures all, its all expends.

So writes W. H. Vanstone in his 'Hymn to the Creator' at the end of *Love's Endeavour, Love's Expense*. With eager hands Christ pours out water to wash the disciples' feet.

With eager heart Christ outpours his life to give to those
who drink the living water.

> Morning glory, starlit sky,
> Leaves in springtime, swallows' flight,
> Autumn gales, tremendous seas,
> Sounds and scents of summer night;
>
> Soaring music, tow'ring words,
> Art's perfection, scholar's truth,
> Joy supreme of human love,
> Memory's treasure, grace of youth;
>
> Open, Lord, are these, thy gifts,
> Gifts of love, to mind and sense;
> Hidden is love's agony,
> Love's endeavour, love's expense.
>
> Love that gives, gives ever more,
> Gives with zeal, with eager hands,
> Spares not, keeps not, all outpours,
> Ventures all, its all expends.
>
> Drained is love in making full;
> Bound in setting others free;
> Poor in making many rich;
> Weak in giving power to be.
>
> Therefore He, Who Thee reveals
> Hangs, O Father, on that Tree
> Helpless; and the nails and thorns
> Tell of what Thy love must be.
>
> Thou art God; no monarch Thou
> Thron'd in easy state to reign;
> Thou art God, Whose arms of love
> Aching, spent, the world sustain.[3]

11

MY SONG IS LOVE

Maundy Thursday (2)

My song is love unknown,
My Saviour's love to me,
Love to the loveless shown
That they might lovely be.[1]

My Saviour's song, which he sings on this night when
Maundy Thursday moves through into Good Friday, is a
song of love, and as each verse succeeds another the depth
and breadth of that love is wonderfully shown.

'My song is love.' Even before the supper, the love has
been shown, when he lays aside his garments and gets
down on his knees and washes their feet and wipes them
with the towel, when he gives them the new commandment, 'Love one another, as I have loved you'. Within
that apostolic band there was a deep fellowship and a
mutual love – love given, love received – and never more
so than on that night of heightened emotions, anticipating
the Passover, about which they fully knew, and fearing
the passion, only half-perceived. There is no night like
this, when Maundy Thursday evening leads into the first
dark hours of Good Friday, in which that fellowship is felt
more strongly in every community of the followers of
Christ. His song is love, love for his disciples, love for the
Church. And in response our song is love, love for our

brothers and sisters, love for the Church, and our shared love for the Lord who first loved us.

'My song is love'. The second verse of Christ's song begins the same. Love at the supper, which we call the last, but only the last until the feasting of the resurrection. They gathered in that upper room, the dark world shut out as they celebrated Passover with bread and wine and Passover songs. If their joy was mingled with foreboding for what lay so close at hand, there was joy none the less, for it was a feast, a party, a family affair for the Lord's adopted family.

And if our own joy is mingled with sorrow, for what we know to await the Lord through the hours of this night, there is joy none the less. There is joy because on Maundy Thursday we meet like them around his table to receive a share, not only in his death, but in his life. There is joy because the Last Supper the Church recalls today became also first Eucharist and a means of grace immeasurable, a source of joy unbounded. There is joy because, for all our sharing in the passion, we look back at the events of this week through the resurrection and know that it is a living Lord who bids us 'do this' to remember him. So, just for a moment, Lent, Holy Week, recede. Joy and sorrow are intermingled now – *Kyrie eleison*, 'Lord, have mercy', but *Gloria in excelsis Deo*, 'Glory to God in the highest' – as they were in that upper room the night he was betrayed. 'My song is love.'

But listen how he sings. Here is a change: 'This is my blood, shed for many' and 'Drink this, all of you'. There is a wideness, a breadth here, that takes you back to the words of Jesus after another great feast, when five thousand had sat down together: 'The bread that I will give for the life of the world is my flesh' (John 6.51). If the washing of feet tells of Christ's love for his disciples, his Church, the scene at the supper, though at first it may seem simply to reinforce that fellowship, in reality opens up what might otherwise be a cosy intimacy. It reveals the love song to be a love song for the whole of humanity. The blood is shed for many, the cup is for all to drink, the bread is for the life of the world.

For all his love for us, for all our love for him, we cannot entrap Jesus Christ within our fellowship. Tomorrow he will stretch out his arms upon the cross that he may embrace all humankind. He recognized in everyone the image – marred, tarnished, but still the image – of God, and so he loved humanity and bids us love our fellows, however different, odd, stubborn or unattractive they may sometimes seem through our vision impaired by sin. His song is love, love for God's children, love for those who reject him, love for the world for which he would die. And, in response, our song is love, love for our fellows, love for the outcast, love for the unloved and unlovely, and loving him, loving Christ, in all of these.

With the bread in his hands, he sings his song of salvation offered to everyone. But how can this bread be for everyone? How can it be shared? Only if it is broken. Here is a truth that the bread he breaks can teach to those who watch him and look for meaning in his every action. This body has to be broken.

It is broken bread that he recognizes as his body. It is broken bread he bids us share. Yes, God in the physical, God in the material, God in a body, but God only in a broken body. That is the heart of the mystery. Our convenience food Eucharists, you with your little rounded personal host and I with mine, obscure the uncomfortable but lovely truth that healing comes when the body is broken. The aesthetic rounded host may be gazed upon, like the baby in the manger, but only the fragmented host, only the broken body, can be given and shared, and thus bring healing and salvation. The broken host, with its jagged edges, with the sharp corners of pain, is what God gives us.

If Christ's song is a love song for the world, then the bread that he breaks and gives is for a broad community composed of 'jagged' people, each with his or her disfigurement, or hurt, or eccentricity or inadequacy. With all that, indeed because of all that, we are the raw material for God's continuing miracle of his presence in the world. We should be suspicious of any Christian community that seems to be a company of the healthy, the whole, the rounded, the pleasing and self-pleasing, the paten of unbroken rounded hosts. For the kingdom is a company of sinners, misfits and ragged, jagged, aching souls. The Church is the company of the broken, and it is the body that is broken – in the upper room, on the cross, at the altar, of the Church – that redeems.

If his song is of love, ours, as at every Eucharist, is our love song to the Broken One, to the Lamb who takes away the sins of the world, *Agnus Dei, qui tollis peccata mundi*. It is the song the Church sings as bread is broken. But it is a song that is a constant challenge to the Church's churchiness, for it hints at a Church where everyone finds mercy and peace, where all may know their sin forgiven, where all may be enfolded in love.

And he, this Broken One, sings on. It is still a love song that he sings, but he sings it now, as the evening moves on, in a different, a minor, key. The supper is over. They sing the psalms of the Passover, as we sing the hymns of the passion. And then into Gethsemane Garden, to the agony and the prayer, 'Abba Father …' Obediently, falteringly at first, but then resolutely, lovingly, he will do the Father's will. 'Not what I want, but what you want' (Mark 14.36). It is a love song for the Father.

At the heart of what we celebrate is the truth that it is

the love of God that we see upon the cross, the generous outpoured, extravagant, divine love, that transforms our weak and possessive, selfish love. For human love is so weak it can deny and retract and fail, as it did in the garden when disciples slept and later fled. His song is love, love for his Father, love for God who is the source of all loving. His song turns out to be God's song, a melody planted deep down in him by his Father, and he will sing it all the way to Calvary.

Christ, the Broken One, sings his love song tonight. Love at the foot-washing – love for the brothers and sisters, love for the Church. Love at the supper – love for the broken, love for the world. Love in the garden – love for the Father, the source of love. Come, then, sing again the timeless song of love, which begins on Maundy Thursday night, and sing on Good Friday quietly, and sing through Saturday night and Sunday triumphantly. Sing the song of love unknown before, a new song, for God is ever at work making all things new:

> My song is love unknown,
> My Saviour's love to me,
> Love to the loveless shown
> That they might lovely be.

12

LAUGHING CRYING MAN

Good Friday (1)

Almighty God,
whose most dear Son went not up to joy
but first he suffered pain,
and entered not into glory before he was crucified:
mercifully grant that we, walking in the way of
the cross,
may find it none other than the way of life and peace;
through Jesus Christ our Lord.[1]

We owe this beautiful and memorable prayer, now the
collect for the Third Sunday of Lent, to an American
divine, William Reed-Huntington, who wrote it in 1882,
drawing for the initial lines on *The Pious and Religious
Consultation* of the sixteenth-century German reformer,
Hermann of Wied.

It presents a picture of Jesus suffering, sorrowful,
broken, this side of the cross; resilient, joyful, glorious on
the other side, the side of the resurrection. There is truth
in that picture, for we have been reflecting on the experiences of a Christ who, while crowds acclaimed him as
king, foresaw a crown of thorns. He was a Christ who,
while sharing with his disciples a supper party at festival
time, saw in the bread they ate a broken body and the wine
they drank blood that would be shed for the forgiveness of

sins. And there is no joy, no resilience, in this world's terms no glory, in the scene in Gethsemane where Jesus struggles with his vocation at its most exacting. 'Father, the Supper's over. Judas is betraying me,' prays the Christ of Elizabeth Jennings' poem, 'Christ's Agony in the Garden'.[2]

> Father, the Supper's over. Judas is
> Betraying me. My Father, I kneel down
> In this dark garden. Now I am helpless.
> It's hard to pray. My God, My Self, my own
> Being, this loneliness
>
> Is too unbearable. Did we ask me
> To live through such? Why, I demand now, why
> Must they be stricken so, why suffer when
> Without free-will, they did not have to die?
> Father, free-will I know
>
> In its full terror. I am sweating here
> Because of liberty. Take time away,
> Show me our Now. My Father help me bear
> All sufferings of all men every day
> And night. Father, the worst pain now's the fear
> That I too shall betray.

In Gethsemane it is all sorrow, all suffering, all broken-ness. We have gone out with Jesus into the dark, into the night.

There is truth in all that. And yet, for a moment, let us look at it another way, and so unearth another truth, as real and as vital as the first. Were Reed-Huntington and Hermann before him quite right when they said 'went not up to joy but first he suffered pain'? Was there no glory, no joy, no laughter this side of the grave? Must the joy belong exclusively to the *alleluia* of Easter? It is only a foreseeing Jesus who is thus portrayed. It is the Jesus who knew every step he would have to take to the cross, every experience he would have to undergo. This is the fore-seeing Jesus, the one with divine foreknowledge of his destiny. And yet the Jesus with precise knowledge is hardly human. And only the really human can be the pattern for the very human me.

Jesus was a man of deep discernment. Of course he had a developed sense of his own destiny. Of course he acquired an all too clear sense of where his vocation would lead. Of course he had an inkling of how the path would lead through desertion and desolation on the way to the death that awaited him. But a Jesus who sails through Holy Week with supernatural knowledge that goes beyond discernment is no saviour for me. The evangelists do us a disservice, albeit an unintentional one, if and when they read back into the teaching and ministry of Jesus precise prediction, even down to the detail of how many days there were to be between death and resurrection. No, death for Jesus must be death indeed with no foreknowledge, least of all of resurrection, though not without faith in God's purposes. And every event in Holy Week must be fully experienced at a human level by a fully human Jesus.

So on Palm Sunday the human Jesus, for all his sense of foreboding, experiences a sense of thrill and exhilaration, as the crowds greet him rapturously. Into the Temple he strides where anger at the abuse of a house of prayer turned into a robbers' den takes hold of him. But then, money changers' tables overturned and tradesmen driven out, he stays, teaching the growing crowd, encouraged, maybe even delighted, by the receptivity of the people with whom his teaching seems to hit home. Then, on Maundy Thursday night, with the washing of the feet and the institution of the Eucharist, there is joy, festivity, cele-bration, fellowship, fun. There is deep fellowship, even for a while security, among his faithful friends, the companions to whom he has grown close.

'Went not up to joy before he suffered pain'? No. He lived life to the full. There was friendship, fellowship, exhilaration, a sort of joy, even in that Holy Week. In its traditional liturgy the Church has responded to that mood, in processions with a hint of carnival on Palm Sunday, and on Maundy Thursday the altar dressed in festal white, *Gloria in excelsis*, 'Glory to God in the highest', silent through Lent, restored to the service, and in every Christian community celebration, festivity, in small measure, and fellowship, friendship, security, among the faithful friends of Christ, the companions who have grown close to him, as the Last Supper is recalled.

But, on Maundy Thursday night, the Church's worship suddenly changes its mood. The Eucharist ended, the altar is stripped, the lights are extinguished, the Church is made bare, the *Gloria in excelsis* seems hours, days, away. On our lips now are the words of the psalmist:

My God, my God, why have you forsaken me?
Why are you so far from helping me, from the words
  of my groaning?
… They divide my clothes among themselves,
and for my clothing they cast lots (Psalm 22.1, 18).

And, if we have any sensitivity in us at all, we hardly wait on Maundy Thursday night to greet our friends, but creep out into the dark, into the night alone.

Why? Because joy has fled. Not gradually, but suddenly, all is confusion. Judas goes out into the dark and we go with him. So does Jesus. He goes with shattered illusions, with friendship betrayed. The faithful turn out to be faithless. They sleep when he bids them pray. They misunderstand and turn to violence, though they have walked three years with the Prince of Peace. They desert him when he looks for a gesture of solidarity. They deny him, like Peter by the fire in the high priest's house, who have previously called him 'Master' and 'Messiah'. And, though John presents us in his Gospel with a Christ whose resolution does not for a moment fail – 'Am I not to drink the cup that the Father has given me?' (John 18.11) – we may be grateful for the earlier evangelists who show a very human Christ in whom the strongest faith is stretched to breaking point:

> Then he withdrew from them about a stone's throw, knelt down, and prayed, 'Father, if you are willing, remove this cup from me; yet, not my will but yours done.' Then an angel from heaven appeared to him and gave him strength. In his anguish he prayed more earnestly, and his sweat became like great drops of blood falling down on the ground (Luke 22.41–44).

And next day on the hillside outside the city, '*Eloi, Eloi, lema sabachthani*. My God, my God, why have you forsaken me?' (Mark 15.34). Thank God for Mark's picture of the human Christ struggling for faith on the cross. For all the dignity and the theological insight of John's portrayal, 'It is finished' (John 19.30), thank God for Mark, and for Christ in despair.

The way of the cross is not the path from sorrow to joy, but the path of suffering and joy, intermingled throughout, though contrasted dramatically as the meal gives way to the prayer in the garden and the long night of arrest and trial. Christianity, the faith in the Crucified One, is a religion for men and women in their strength – exhilarated, encouraged, walking tall – and a religion for men and women in their weakness – broken, disappointed, suffering, brought very low. And for most of us it is a religion for those who know strength and weakness, and seek God equally in both experiences. If we follow Jesus along the path he has chosen to tread, we cannot but perceive his laughter and his tears. We see the companionable man of fellowship who is sometimes most dreadfully alone. We enter into the mind of one clear in his discernment, yet suddenly lost, of one unfailingly articulate who suddenly speaks not a word. We see him in his strength and yet we also share his weakness.

> Laughing, crying
> man of fellowship,
> strong in weakness,
> lost, now left alone.

That is authentic humanity. And it is something like that path that God invites all who would follow Christ to walk.

So we have been brought to the climax of it all. We have recalled the steps along the way – waving of palms, washing of feet, breaking of bread, sharing of wine, desertion of friends. We have come to the hour of the passion. But still the paradox is unresolved and will continue to be until the end of time. Still defeat and glory go hand in hand, joy and sorrow are bound together. 'My God, my God, why have you forsaken me?' Yet 'It is finished.' Crucified criminal, yet triumphant king.

Unresolved until the end of time? Unresolved certainly until we see the vision of God. What will we see then? The unutterable beauty, the disfigurement melted away? Christians have seen in Isaiah's suffering servant an uncanny prefiguring of the Broken One on the cross.

> He had no form or majesty that we should look at him,
> nothing in his appearance that we should desire him.
> He was despised and rejected by others;
> a man of suffering and acquainted with infirmity;
> and as one from whom others hide their faces
> he was despised, and we held him of no account
> (Isaiah 53.2b–3).

Will that all have melted away or still, in the embrace of the Father, will we find ourselves touched by hands that are scarred for all eternity? Is the paradox deep within the heart of God, whom we want to be impassible, but need to share our pain?

But in the meantime, while we have before us not the vision of God in heaven, but the stark cross of the Broken One, however much we may believe that the one scene may illuminate the other, what shall we do? Gaze? There is a limited usefulness to gazing, though for a while it may bring wonder and deep thankfulness. Christians sometimes imagine that where they stand on Good Friday is at the foot of the cross, determined to be like Mary and John, and more faithful than those who ran away. Indeed they can sometimes imagine their task is to be in the shoes, so to speak, of almost anybody in the passion drama except the Lord himself. They can look at the cross through the eyes of a Roman official, or a soldier, or a disciple, of Peter from a distance, or John closer to the cross. But that is to miss the point.

The point is to be, not at the foot of the cross or a distance away, but on it. The point is not to identify with Pilate or Peter or Mary, but to identify with Christ, to share the paradox that does nothing to dull his pain, and to look out at the world from the cross with the love that brought him there and kept him there, though he felt deserted, till all is accomplished. The end of the sorrowful way is to be up there with him, finding it has been the path of life and peace. That is why it is so good that Holy Communion on Good Friday has been restored by the new liturgies – communion for the whole congregation, bread and wine – enabling us to recognize on that day of all days that, as Paul puts it, 'as often as you eat the bread and drink the cup, you proclaim the Lord's death until he comes' (1 Corinthians 11.26). When in the liturgy of

Good Friday we stop gazing and get up out of our places to receive the broken bread and the cup of wine, it is our way of sharing his passion, the paradox and the pain. We will not simply gaze at the cross. We will be conformed to it. We will accept its constraints. We will see the world from its perspective. We will discover its mysterious power for our lives and for the whole human race.

Like the penitent thief, we will keep company with the Lord.

> Laughing, crying
> man of fellowship,
> strong in weakness,
> crucified criminal, triumphant king.

13

LADY OF SORROWS

Good Friday (2)

Christians often find it helpful to meditate on the 'seven words from the cross'. It is an approach that has its problems, for the different gospel writers are making quite different theological points by the words they record on the lips of the dying Christ. When we draw them all together in a coherent sequence, we deprive them of some of their power. But let us stay with John, with his words of Christ from the cross, with no hint of Mark's cry of dereliction. Here is a Christ who draws the world to himself, triumphs from the cross, and utters only words that accord with that theological perspective.

> When Jesus saw his mother and the disciple whom he loved standing beside her, he said to his mother, 'Woman, here is your son.' Then he said to the disciple, 'Here is your mother.' And from that hour the disciple took her into his own home (John 19.26–27).

It is one of the sad ironies of the Christian religion that in his passion Jesus bequeathed to the Church a person and an ordinance, and we have made both a source of contention. The ordinance is the Eucharist, the person Mary his mother. Over the Eucharist, which shows forth so powerfully in broken bread and shared cup the meaning of God's reconciliation, we have fought battles through Christian history. About Mary, whom the Lord gives to the Church as mother, Christians have so often fallen out and misunderstood both Jesus and one another.

Here is Mary, standing at the foot of the cross, with the Beloved Disciple, whom we take to be John, in whose Gospel alone the story is recorded, so that it has an eyewitness quality about it. We usually understand these words from the cross as more than simply evidence that Jesus left things in good order before he died and made sure his mother would be looked after, as a dutiful son would do. We usually see the Beloved Disciple as representative of the Church, so that Jesus is giving his mother not to an individual, but to the Christian community.

What does it mean for the church to have Mary as a mother? Mary is the model of purity, of that unfashionable virtue virginity, and sometimes Christians have made a lot of that part of her witness. But I suspect that is not what the Scriptures are interested in. Mary is also the model of obedience. At the annunciation her 'Be it unto me according to your word' is the key to the incarnation. And, yes, that is important. But we lose the essential gift of Mary to the Church if we only look to the story of Christ's birth.

The crucial text of Scripture that links birth and death, for Mary and her son, is of course that prophecy of old Simeon, forty days after Christmas when the child is brought to the Temple, that the child is destined for the falling and rising of many in Israel, to be a sign that will be rejected, and that a sword will pierce Mary's own soul also. The way of Mary, as for her son, is the way of the cross.

When those infancy tales are over, we do not hear of her again until the cross, except hovering on the edge of the scene, with her other children, quite ambivalent about Jesus, wondering whether they should not take him home, and being rebuffed by him because they did not understand, whether it was at a wedding feast or when he was casting out devils.

But there she is at the cross, and she does not say a word.

One of the most powerful Good Friday images that has stayed in my memory is from back in the early 1980s when television screens were showing violent scenes outside and on top of prisons – it was the Holy Week of the Strangeways riots and all that built around that. They were very masculine scenes that have stuck in my mind. Prisoners or their guards, politicians or commentators – a male world, harsh, brutal, tough. And Calvary was in many respects like that. But in the middle of that prison picture we sometimes saw women. Most of them were mothers. They were brought in to urge their sons, upon the roof, to come down. They were the Marys of the scene staring up at their convict sons. The Marys of the scene – but not quite. For Mary stood at the foot of the cross, with her few female companions, in this masculine scene, in all its harshness, brutality and clamour, but – and this is the crucial thing – she did not ask him to come down. She did not ask him to come down; she simply stood her ground.

She had learned, little by little maybe, gradually, not to want to take him home, not to want to get him down, but to let him fulfil his vocation. She had learned by staying with him what he must do. He must be about his Father's business. But it was indeed like a sword through her soul.

Above all else Mary seems to me to be the model of faithfulness, even more than purity, even more than obedience, faithfulness. And I suspect that it has its reward, not just in being the woman 'clothed with the sun, with the moon under her feet, and on her head a crown of twelve stars,' as the Revelation to John pictures it (12.1), but in her beginning to understand. Mary did not urge him to come down, because she was beginning to understand.

Mary the model of faithfulness, the model for those who stay with the Church, who stay with the faith, who stick to prayer, who live by discipline, and perhaps not until the end of their lives begin to understand the deep mysteries of the things of God. She whom some Christians call 'Our Lady of Sorrows' can teach us this, as her Son, hanging on his cross, gives her to us as a mother.

She stands there as he, knowing that all was now finished, said (to fulfil the Scripture) 'I am thirsty' (John 19.28). She at whose breast he had drunk life-giving milk, she who had seen him turn water into wine to satisfy the wedding guests, is powerless now to give him even a cup of water. Here is another of those ironies of the passion. Christ is the one who gives living water. Christ is the one who turns water into wine. Christ is the one who offers a cup as a sign of sharing his life and his death, and now he himself is thirsty; and all that they will offer him is a bitter drink.

It is only John who gives us this word from the cross, and with John things are never as straightforward as they look. We are not just being given these words to indicate that Jesus felt parched and faint, for John of all the evangelists is least interested in the suffering of the cross. What we have here is a pointer to the means by which Christians are joined with Christ, in the thirst assuaged both in baptism and in Eucharist. His Gospel is rich in imagery to draw us back to those two great sacramental signs.

Remember the baptismal imagery at the foot-washing – 'those who have bathed need no further washing'. And so it will be later with blood and water as they pierce the side of the lifeless body (John 19.34). And now Jesus cries out from the cross, 'I am thirsty'. Here is a plea addressed to you and to me for what we might call 'sacramental union', a deep fellowship with him through baptism. He wants to share the living water with all those who have been through the water of baptism, and in so doing have accepted his pattern of dying and rising, death and resurrection.

In baptism the Christian, signed with the cross, is joined to Christ in his death and in his resurrection. As the Second Letter to Timothy puts it, 'If we have died with him, we shall live with him; if we hold firm, we shall reign with him' (2 Timothy 2.11). What is promised and inaugurated in baptism is nothing less than what was promised and inaugurated when James and John responded to that crucial question that Jesus put to them and which re-echoes through every occasion of Christian baptism: 'Are you willing to be baptized with the baptism with which I am baptized?' (Mark 10.38). It is as if Christ, who is thirsty for your fellowship, calls you up to the cross to share it with him.

He wants to share the cup of salvation with all those who, by sharing in the Eucharist, show forth his death. He wants those who take broken bread into their hands to share his brokenness. He wants those who say too glibly 'We offer you our souls and bodies to be a living sacrifice' to make a costly offering of themselves that joins them to his eternal sacrifice upon the altar of the cross. To all who will hear he puts this question that he put to James and John: 'Are you willing to drink the cup that I am drinking?' He wants you to answer 'Yes'. For Christ, who is thirsty for this sacramental union with you that baptism and Eucharist both act out, calls you up to the cross to share.

She shares it, the Lady of Sorrows, her faithfulness never faltering, sharing his cup of suffering as Simeon had warned she would. And then she hears him speak again. 'It is finished', and she sees him bow his head and give up his spirit.

It is finished. The ordeal is over. He has gone through it all, save death itself, and that is now to take him over. He has walked the sorrowful way with passion, and it is over. It is finished.

Yet it is more than that. The Greek has something of the sense of 'It is accomplished', 'It is consummated'. Something has been achieved, something immeasurable, something eternal, something that changes the whole relationship of the human race to its creator. Paul tells us that 'God reconciled us to himself in Christ' (2 Corinthians 5.18), and, though that process begins in the pain of giving birth in the stable at Bethlehem, it reaches its climax on the hill outside Jerusalem in the pain of life-giving death.

It is because, for John, the cross is all accomplishment – it is not disaster, or failure, or tragedy, it is the will of God, it is the means of the world's salvation, it is good news, gospel, for the human race – that his account of the life and death of Jesus Christ is all about glory, but glory of a strange divine sort that the world fails to perceive. Jesus's path through life is a triumphal procession revealing the glory of God, and the cross is the grand climax, where the ultimate victory is won. 'I, when I am lifted up from earth, will draw all people to myself!' (John 12.32).

In the liturgy of Good Friday, for all its solemnity, for all the tears that get suppressed or shed, there is a quiet confidence and more than a hint of glory. We wait for Easter when the Risen Lord will be among us in power, but we know that his victory does not delay till then. It is won high upon the cross, the world drawn to him, divine nature revealed, and humankind reconciled to God.

She stands there, this Lady of Sorrows. She sees her son, her Saviour, die. Does she understand, at least a little? Perhaps. For she stands there. Like her son at his trial she does not say a word. Not for a moment does she ask him to come down. He must accomplish his Father's business. And it has been accomplished, so thirsty souls may drink the new wine of the kingdom.

14

THE MEANING IS IN THE WAITING

Easter Eve

One of the subtleties of Holy Week is the way that the liturgy each day has a twist at the end that moves our meditating, thinking and praying on to a new phase. On Palm Sunday we are not allowed to go away still waving palms and singing our hosannas. We read the passion and move on so that the mood of Maundy Thursday and Good Friday is almost upon us. And then, on Maundy Thursday itself, we are not allowed to slip home full of the warm glow of the fellowship in the upper room, but are confronted with the darkness and the night, the desolation and the betrayal.

What is the mood that we take home on Good Friday? Of course we take home the cross, with its shame and glory, and all the deep emotions we bring to the surface as we celebrate the passion. But, in a sense, what we also have to take is the space, the yawning gap, between that three o'clock on Friday afternoon and that event in the darkness of the night that links Saturday and Sunday, before dawn, when mysteriously, unwatched by human eyes, the Lord bursts the grave. That space, that yawning gap, has no liturgy. There is nothing, save the Church's daily prayer and Scripture reading, from the moment we celebrate the Lord's death until the moment when we celebrate his resurrection. It is significant that there is nothing, but it is important that the nothingness be not passed over. The yawning gap has its own part to play in our story. I often puzzle over it, the meaning of Jesus dead and buried, the meaning for his disciples with no thought of the resurrection, but also the meaning for him.

The First Letter of Peter also puzzles over it:

> He was put to death in the flesh, but made alive in the spirit, in which also he went and made a proclamation to the spirits in prison (1 Peter 3.18b–19a).

The Creed affirms something of the same truth, insisting, perhaps a little misleadingly, that 'he descended into hell'. Christian theology, at least in medieval times, developed that into a picture of a Christ who 'harrows hell', who descends into hell and defeats the powers of evil; it is a favourite theme of art and drama in the Middle Ages. Here, of course, we are not only into a highly pictorial language, but into an area of speculation, unable to speak with precision about the nature of things the other side of death. But I suggest that some of the meaning of the space, the yawning gap, is in the waiting.

R. S. Thomas has a lovely poem, not intended for Holy Saturday, but appropriate for it, about the meaning found in the waiting:

> Moments of great calm,
> Kneeling before an altar
> Of wood in a stone church
> In summer, waiting for the God
> To speak; the air a staircase
> For silence; the sun's light
> Ringing me, as though I acted
> A great role. And the audiences
> Still; all that close throng
> Of spirits waiting, as I,
> For the message.

97

Prompt me, O God;
But not yet. When I speak,
Though it be you who speak
Through me, something is lost.
The meaning is in the waiting.[1]

Enter, if you can, imaginatively into the mind of
Christ. He has endured. He has accomplished. Death has
done its worst and darkness has overwhelmed his soul.
Does the desolation he has known in this life follow him
to Hades? What is it like for Christ in the place of the
dead? We cannot know, at least not entirely. But we are
not without clue. For in our human life we do experience
moments of deep darkness that we believe are death-like.
The end of a dream, the death of a loved one, a broken
marriage or love affair, a painful ending to a friendship,
even the loss of faith. All these are moments when life
stands still, empty of meaning, robbed of all its familiarity
and security. We are utterly exposed. That is the nearest
most of us have ever come to an experience of death. And
our exposure, our vulnerability and our numbness is a
kind of nakedness akin to the nakedness of Christ as they
took his bruised and broken body down from the cross.
There is too a kind of nakedness of the soul.

In those experiences of darkness there is at first a sort of
nothingness, an emptiness, a numbness. There is not even
the desire to live again, to flourish again. There is no
thought, to speak theologically, of resurrection. It is total
darkness, not just darkness over the land, but darkness in
the soul.

But there does come salvation, there does come hope,
sometimes long delayed, sometimes more speedily than
we could have dreamed. Rarely is it instant. At first it is
the smallest flickering light, the sense that we might come
through; no more than that. But, almost imperceptibly

often, something spells a glimmer of hope. A word from a friend, or even a stranger, a gesture of affection or compassion, a touch, a change of surroundings, a powerful remembering, a flood of tears. One of these, or something like it, introduces the possibility of new life, fresh beginning. The waiting has started. It is not that 'salvation' has arrived. It may be far away, and still long delayed. But the possibility has been perceived and there is something on which to build.

Much later on – days, weeks, months, even years later – we discover healing, wholeness, restoration. We realize that a burden has been lifted from us. Sometimes it is that we have learned to live with the situation, and with some senses of loss perhaps that is as far as we can go. But there are circumstances when something more fundamental can happen. There is a chance that we might call it 'resurrection', but, unless we are very theological beings, we probably do not. We say instead 'I've got over it now'. But, looking back, we can recognize, perhaps, that the point of growth, of new maturity, of deepened self-understanding, or even of religious conviction, was neither the point of desolation, which was totally negative and destructive, nor the point of realization of healing, which was the moment of celebration and joy, but the long wait, at first in the dark and then in the slowly growing light. It is in the reflection, or the questioning, or the patience, or the longing of the waiting that we find, or find anew, both God and our true selves. 'The meaning is in the waiting.'

In Holy Week we tend to look at Jesus and, by rehearsing his story once again, to discover connections that make sense of our own. As we look at the lifeless body of the Saviour and the near silence of Scripture and liturgy on the meaning of his being dead, we have to approach this part of the story of our redemption from the other end, so to speak. We have to begin with ourselves, and that process of dying and rising through the traumas and crises of human existence, and ask 'And was it like this for him?' In the experience of death, in the descending into hell, as the creed puts it, was there for him the recovery of faith, the waiting and the yearning for the Father to act, the sense of light at the end of the tunnel, before ever the realization that the tunnel was but a tomb, and the love of the Father was stronger than death? Did he cry out, as we do sometimes, 'How long, O Lord, how long?' Was it like this for Jesus as it was for Job?

> Oh, that you would hide me in Sheol,
> that you would conceal me until your wrath is past,
> that you would appoint me a set time, and remember me!
> If mortals die, will they live again?
> All the days of my service I would wait until my
> release should come (Job 14.13–14).

I do not know. But I suspect something like it if we are to make sense of the space and the yawning gap.

So we come back from the experience of Jesus to ourselves, and recognize how important it is that Easter Eve is not just a day off between Good Friday and Easter Day, but is the day of waiting, as crucial as the day of dying and the day of rising. The silence between the shout of 'Crucify' and the 'Alleluia' song is more than a void. The silence is as significant as the song.

Of course, waiting has been a feature of the whole story of the passion. The authorities waiting for a chance to take Jesus. Judas waiting for an opportunity to betray him. Peter and John hovering on the edge of the trial. Mary waiting for her son's pain to end, even if hers could not die with his. Soldiers waiting to get the execution over and the body taken away. The other Mary waiting for the first signs of dawn so that she might go to the tomb. And

Jesus, waiting to die that all might be accomplished, waiting to die that all the world might be drawn to himself, waiting in death, perhaps, for the love of the Father to overcome death. Always there is waiting. Always within the waiting the seeds of new life. The meaning so often is in the waiting.

We must not be afraid of the long unspectacular waitings of which much of life is made up, nor must we be too urgent for the coming of every Easter in our lives, lest we fail to learn from the silence before the first *alleluia* breaks forth. Think of Jesus, in the place of the departed, waiting for his salvation to come. Let the waiting teach us through its long silences the infinite patience of God.

15

WHEN YOU PASS THROUGH THE WATERS

Easter

All night had shout of men and cry
Of woeful women filled his way;
Until that noon of sombre sky
On Friday, clamour and display
Smote him; no solitude had he,
No silence, since Gethsemane.

Public was Death; but Power, but Might,
But life again, but Victory,
Were hushed within the dead of night,
The shuttered dark, the secrecy.
And all alone, alone, alone,
He rose again behind the stone.[1]

Alice Meynell's evocative poem affirms the truth that the resurrection belongs to the dark of the night. Too often Easter can be portrayed as a festival of the morning, preferably an English spring morning, with sunshine and daffodils. And indeed that can bring joy to the heart and the joy interacts with the good news that Christ is risen. But there is a danger if we lose sight of the fact that the resurrection comes out of the darkness, the blackness, and the Christian who wants to sense what that means does well to share in the ancient Easter Liturgy, that begins, at least, in darkness, whether on Saturday night, already the third day by Jewish reckoning where the day begins with dusk, or in the early pre-dawn hours of Sunday morning. It has been an extraordinary deprivation for many Christians through centuries that that powerful Easter Liturgy has been misunderstood, or side-lined or even unknown. Equally, now that it is once again establishing itself as a central celebration in the liturgical life of so many churches, it is a source of fresh insight and blessing.

Christians find their way into the darkened church. When last they came it was a church stripped of colour and ornament, made bare for Good Friday. In the dark one can not be sure whether all that has changed. There is a scent in the air that was not there on Good Friday and more than a suspicion that, when the church is filled with light, it will prove to be very different. Indeed those who have slaved away in the church all day making it ready for Easter will know that to be the case. People come with a sense of anticipation. No, it is not Easter yet, but almost so. They have been waiting, and waiting has turned into anticipation. The power, the might, the life again, the victory are near, hidden within the dead of night, the shuttered dark, the secrecy. That is the mood as they wait for the liturgy to begin and then through its opening stages, reading the Scriptures and praying, singing and keeping silence in the dark.

The first focus of the liturgy is fire and light. From the 'new fire' the paschal flame is kindled, the great candle that stands for the Risen Christ. It is an Easter symbol that will burn through the paschal season, night and day, and have its place in the broad daylight of Easter morning. But of course its first lighting and the first proclamation of its message belongs to the night. It is light in the darkness, the light of the risen Christ for the darkness of the world and of the human soul.

But the Easter Liturgy does not remain focused on the

light, though the paschal candle still towers above the celebration. Once the church is in light and the Scriptures have been proclaimed, the focus moves to the font, full to the brim with water. It may be that the font stands in the midst of the people. Or it may be that they have to get up and walk, yet another of those little pilgrimages that reflect the Christian journey, to come to the font in some corner of the church. Either way they gather there, the font, or, more precisely, the water, the focus now of their celebration. But why the water? What has water got to do with Easter night and Easter morning?

They will have some idea by the time they reach this moment. For the vigil of Scripture readings through which they will have come will have had water as its most prominent theme. They will have heard – it will have served as a kind of biblical text for all that follows – the account of creation from Genesis:

> In the beginning when God created the heavens and the earth, the earth was a formless void and darkness covered the face of the deep, while a wind from God swept over the face of the waters (1.1–2).

There it is, right at the beginning of Scripture, right at the beginning of all things, the deep, the water, and hovering over the water the Spirit of God, in relationship with his creation. Expectations are raised. There follow water stories that fulfil those expectations, stories in which the water is the place of encounter with God.

The first is the story of the flood, of Noah, and of the ark; the ark in which, as the writer of 1 Peter puts it, 'a few, that is, eight persons, were saved through water' (3.20). It is an odd phrase, 'through water', for in the plain meaning of the story Noah, his wife, his sons and his sons' wives, were not saved through water, but from water. But the confusion, if confusion it be, will turn out to be important. Certainly for Noah there is encounter with God as the ark provides its refuge from the flood that has covered the earth. The encounter, for all that it is one that reveals the severity of God towards wrongdoing, is also a moment of revelation of the graciousness of God:

> I have set my bow in the clouds, and it shall be a sign of the covenant between me and the earth. When I bring clouds over the earth and the bow is seen in the clouds, I will remember my covenant that is between me and you and every living creature of all flesh; and the waters shall never again become a flood to destroy all flesh (Genesis 9.13–15).

The encounter establishes a covenant. The water spells salvation, not only for the eight in the ark, but, in a sense, for all humankind.

But then there comes the next great story of the water, in the escape of the Israelite people from the land of Egypt through the waters of the Red Sea. And here again, as in the story of the flood, the water is the place of destruction for those who have offended God. The Egyptian horses and their riders he has thrown into the sea. But the Israelites pass through the waters dry-shod. It is a story of extraordinary power; for the Israelite people the story *par excellence* of their rescue and salvation. In a sense they go through the water, they pass through the sea, but the sea is swept back to let them through; it stands high above them all, a wall to right and to left. Again, in one sense they are saved from the water, from its destructive power, and yet, again, they speak of it as salvation by the water and through the water, for they pass through the walls of water, and the enemy perishes in the water; they are saved from Pharaoh's hosts by the water. Once again there is an encounter with God, with a God of severity and destruc-

tion, but who is also a God of graciousness to those whom
he has chosen, and a God of promise, leading them on,
albeit through the wilderness, to a land of milk and honey.

The third great story of the deep, not so often heard at
the Easter Liturgy today but part of the ancient provision
for this vigil, is the tale of Jonah and his whale. 'You cast
me into the deep, into the heart of the seas,' says Jonah in
his pleading prayer to the Lord, 'and the flood surrounded
me; all your waves and billows passed over me' (Jonah
2.3). The pattern now established, it is no surprise to
discover that the water is not so much the place of Jonah's
destruction, but of his encounter. The Spirit of God still
moves over the waters and there is a remaking of a
covenant, so that Jonah is spewed out on the shore so that
he may set out for Nineveh to make his proclamation.
This time wicked men and women are saved. Jonah's
shipmates throw him into the sea, at his request, so that
they may be saved. By his sacrifice, they escape. By his
encounter in the deep, he also is rescued and set back on
course. But, most importantly, his experience sends him
to Nineveh, and so the people there repent of their
wickedness, and do not perish. Once again, by the water
and through the water, salvation is established.

When it comes to the New Testament, the Easter
Liturgy abandons the water imagery; not surprisingly for
the gospel reading must be an account of the resurrection.
But, staying with it for a moment, it is worth looking at
the two significant stories of Jesus and his disciples on the
water. In the first, Jesus stills the storm, which threatened
to upset the boat and send the disciples into the sea. It is a
moment of encounter and, of course, it is one of those
moments that place Jesus where an earlier, Old Testament, understanding would have put only God. The
encounter with the one who stills the storm, who controls
the elements, who brings peace and calm, is not with an

invisible Holy One, such as Noah, Moses or Jonah experienced. This encounter is with a man, but a man in whom is God. The Jesus whom the disciples knew so well became himself an encounter with the living God, and in the encounter there was salvation. They were saved from the water.

There is another story when the disciples were once again in a boat, but this time without the Lord, until they encountered him, coming to them, as Matthew tells it, walking on the water. Peter, seeing the Lord, jumps into the water, and then, losing nerve, faith failing, finds himself in danger of being swallowed up in the deep. And in the encounter with Christ he is rescued. He is saved from the water. The story has an uncanny echo of one of the great resurrection appearances that John recounts. There the Lord stands on the shore, rather than on the water, but the action of Peter is the same. Seeing the Lord, he jumps into the water. In John's version there is no moment of danger. In the end, of course, there turns out to be no danger in the version that Matthew has told. Always the Lord is in control. Always the water is the place, not of destruction, but of salvation.

There is, of course, a crucial word in the Christian vocabulary that is never mentioned in any of these stories, but which relates to them, if not in their original telling, at least in the way Christians have done their theology with the stories. The word is 'baptism'. The Christian is saved from a kind of drowning by baptism – saved from the water. The Christian encounters the saving Lord in the waters of baptism – saved by or through the water. Thus for Christians the escape from Egypt through the waters of the Red Sea is seen as a prefiguring of baptism. The Israelites come through the waters, seeking rescue and salvation, and arrive eventually in the promised land. The Christian comes through the waters of baptism, seeking rescue and salvation, and is initiated into the Church. The Christian in baptism, like Peter sinking into the deep, encounters the Lord in the waters and is safe.

Even the Lord himself does not escape being drawn into this water imagery. 'Through the deep waters of death you brought your Son,' says the baptismal liturgy.[2] There is at least a threefold parallelism: the Israelite goes through a life-threatening experience in the Red Sea, but comes through to the Promised Land; the Lord goes through a life-destroying experience on the cross (the deep waters of death), but comes through to the life of the resurrection; the Christian goes through the water of baptism, with its message of dying and rising, but comes to the secure haven of the Church and of the kingdom.

All of that is present as the Church gathers around the font at Easter. This is the place of rebirth, a kind of womb, Christians coming to birth in the breaking of the waters. But the font is, Easter night teaches, also a kind of tomb, yet a tomb that does not give an opposite message. For the tomb, as much as the womb, spells new life, rebirth, resurrection. So, at the font, the Church prays over the water, baptizes new Christians and invites the whole company of the baptized to renew their baptismal commitment. For baptism is not so much something that happened once upon a time as the beginning of a calling to a particular style of life. It is not so much that we were baptized in the past, but that we are baptized in the present. We live out our baptism every day. We make it our own by use. And we reclaim it, supremely in the Easter Liturgy.

Baptism commits us to life in the fellowship of the baptized community. It commits us to life in relationship with a generous God showering gifts, some of them unexpected, some of them not quite what we would have asked for. It commits us to a life that keeps coming back for forgiveness and new beginnings, and never falling away into self-despair. It commits us to a life where the baptismal relationship is renewed in the Eucharist. It commits us to a life where water keeps being turned into wine. It commits us to a life open to the Spirit who dwells within and yet who also comes like a new gift ever fresh. Most of all it commits us to a pattern of life and death and life again, a pattern of dying and rising, that reverses the world's wisdom that thinks it foolishness, a Christ-like pattern that defies the conventional and finds glory where you least expect it.

All that, and more, is what baptism means for the Christian. It is the baptism with which we go on being baptized. And what a way of life it is, a sorrowful way and a road to salvation, almost impossible, but, for those who have heard the call, quite irresistible.

The Christ of Alice Meynell's poem moves from death to life in secret and alone. For all the glad company of the Church, and the fellowship of the baptized, there is a reserve that properly allows us to walk our disciple's path with some things hidden, not least some of the pain, though please God some inarticulated joys as well, and there is also a sense in which we have sometimes to be alone. To walk Christ's way is sometimes to walk in isolation. If it is to be his way, sometimes it will be so isolated that the truth that Christ knows what is hidden and that Christ walks alongside will be part of what we cannot sense. But at least some of the time we shall be able to hear the words of Isaiah that become those of the Lord himself:

Do not fear, for I have redeemed you;
I have called you by name, you are mine.
When you pass through the waters, I will be with you
    (Isaiah 43.1b–2a).

There are Christians, but not all, who are blessed with a constant sense of the companionship of Christ. For them there is never the sense of being alone. He is present in every moment and circumstance. For most that overwhelming sense of his presence is less constant. We sense it in worship when a community is open to the Risen Lord in word and bread and fellowship, as by the lakeside or on the road to Emmaus and around the table at the journey's end.

Each such sense of presence is an extension of the presence, which is more like encounter, that we experience in the Easter Liturgy itself. When that liturgy is celebrated with all its dramatic power, the presence of the Risen Christ, bursting the grave, offering life, breathing in the Spirit, calling by name, draws out of us recognition, faith and joy that can carry us a long way. But the depth of our recognition, our faith and our joy will depend on how truly we have been walking with him the sorrowful way, both liturgically through Lent, and also, more fundamentally, through the whole business of living openly and with integrity in God's world. Where there has been, and will continue to be, real identification (and baptism has committed us to nothing less) there will be a profound experience of reunion, communion, with the Risen One. The resurrection will be implanted deep within us.

Not only at Easter, but at other times resurrection images will come to our aid and fill us with joy. It may be that sometimes Christ seems to plunge into the water ahead of us, calling us to follow as he leaps in and swims for the distant bank. There is nowhere we need to go where he has not been first. It may be that sometimes he seems to beckon from the shore, ready to issue that invitation that we have heard repeatedly: 'Come, and eat.' [3] There we recognize him, the Risen One, in the breaking of the bread. It may be that sometimes he seems to stand there radiantly alive, with the glorious scars on the feet that have walked the sorrowful way and on the hands that are always open ready to embrace. We may know that we have only half understood what it means to be baptized with his baptism, that we have a long way to go before we are conformed to his image, that we hardly know what we mean when, with Peter, we say 'Lord, you know that I love you.' But in response, reliably and repeatedly, we hear again the gracious call, 'Follow me. Take up your cross and follow me', and know it to be the path of life.

1 Conformed to the Image of his Son

1. The Alternative Service Book 1980, p. 131.

2 Led all that Way for Birth or Death?

1. W. H. Auden, 'At the Manger Mary sings', *Collected Longer Poems*, Faber & Faber, 1968.
2. T. S. Eliot, 'The Journey of the Magi', *Collected Poems 1909–1962*, Faber & Faber, 1963.
3. H. J. Hopkins, 'We Three Kings', in *The Oxford Book of Carols*, Oxford University Press, 1964.

3 How Long they had Waited

1. The Apostles' Creed (*Book of Common Prayer*).
2. William Walsham How, 'Who is this so weak and helpless?' *The New English Hymnal*, Canterbury Press, 1994.
3. *The Promise of His Glory*, Mowbray/Church House Publishing, 1991, pp. 281f.
4. *Lent, Holy Week, Easter*, SPCK, 1986, pp. 229f.

4 No Ordinary Time

1. T. S. Eliot, *Murder in the Cathedral*, Faber & Faber, 1935.
2. The Alternative Service Book 1980, p. 130.
3. Ibid. p. 132.
4. Ibid. p. 137.
5. Ibid. p. 138.
6. Ibid. p. 231.
7. Ibid. p. 138.
8. Ibid. p. 125.

6 Bread instead of Ashes

1. *Lent, Holy Week, Easter*, SPCK, 1986, p. 26.
2. The Alternative Service Book 1980, p. 316.
3. Elizabeth Jennings, 'Bread', *In the Meantime*, Carcanet Press, 1996.

7 Finding the True Cross

1. The Alternative Service Book 1980, pp. 136, 137 and 141.
2. Ibid. p. 131.

8 Making Connections

1. Dorothy L. Sayers, *The Just Vengeance*, Gollancz, 1946; the quotation forms the opening of the Doctrine Commission Report, *Believing in the Church*, 1981.
2. *Lent, Holy Week, Easter*, SPCK, 1986, p. 77.

9 Are You a King?

1. *The Coronation Rite of HM Queen Elizabeth II*, Novello, 1953, p. 65.
2. Christina Rossetti, 'The Love of Christ that passeth knowledge', *The Works of Christina Rossetti*, Wordsworth, 1995.

10 Bowl and Font and Spear

1. Edwin le Grice, 'Image of the eternal Father', *Sing Together*, Canterbury Press, 1994.
2. James Quinn, 'God is love', *The New English Hymnal*, Canterbury Press, 1994.
3. W. H. Vanstone, 'A Hymn to the Creator', *Love's Endeavour, Love's Expense*, Darton, Longman and Todd, 1977.

11 My Song is Love

1. Samuel Crossman, 'My song is love unknown', *The New English Hymnal*, Canterbury Press, 1994.

12 Laughing Crying Man

1. The Alternative Service Book 1980, p. 512.
2. Elizabeth Jennings, 'Christ's Agony in the Garden', *Consequently I Rejoice*, Carcanet Press, 1977.

14 The Meaning is in the Waiting

1. R. S. Thomas, 'Kneeling', *Selected Poems, 1948–1968*, Hart-Davis, MacGibbon, 1973.

15 When You Pass through the Waters

1. Alice Meynell, 'Easter Night', *Collected Poems*, Burns & Oates, 1923.
2. The Alternative Service Book 1980, p. 231.
3. John 21.12, author's translation.